# Lawrence At Tregerthen

D. H. Lawrence

Lawrence At Tregerthen

(D. H. Lawrence in Cornwall)

by

C. J. Stevens

The Whitston Publishing Company
Troy, New York
1988

I dedicate this book to Stanley Hocking, in memory.

# Contents

# Acknowledgments

I owe a special debt of gratitude to Stanley Hocking, Kitty Rogers, Ivor Short, H. H. Hocking, P. O. Eddy, Mary Hocking, Arthur Eddy, and John Hocking.

To John Martin, Emile Delavenay, Warren Roberts, Kate Nicholson, and James C. Cowan for information and suggestions.

To Studio St. Ives, Ltd., Evan A. and Doreen Blandford for photographs, and Thomson Newspapers, Ltd.

To *The D. H. Lawrence Review* in which some of the Stanley Hocking material first appeared.

Acknowledgments are made to the following publishers for the material from the books indicated:

Anchor Books, *The Selected Letters of D. H. Lawrence,* ed. by Diana Trilling.

Boni & Liveright, *I Have This to Say: The Story of my Flurried Years,* by Violet Hunt.

Cambridge University Press, *The Letters of D. H. Lawrence,* Vol. II, ed. by George J. Zytaruk & James T. Boulton; and Vol. III, ed. by James T. Boulton & Andrew Robertson.

Jonathan Cape, *Peter Warlock: A Memoir of Philip Heseltine,* by Cecil Gray; and *Reminiscences of D. H. Lawrence,* by John Middleton Murry.

Doubleday & Company, Inc., *The Poet H. D. and Her World,* by Barbara Guest.

Farrar, Straus and Giroux, *The Priest of Love,* a revised and enlarged edition of *The Intelligent Heart,* by Harry T. Moore.

Harcourt, Brace and Company, Inc., *The Flowers of the Forest,* by David Garnett.

William Heinemann, Ltd., *The Collected Letters of D. H. Lawrence,* Vol. 1 & 2, ed. by Harry T. Moore; and *The Memoirs and Correspondences,* by Frieda Lawrence, ed. by E. W. Tedlock.

Alfred A. Knopf, Inc., *Lorenzo in Taos,* by Mabel Dodge Luhan; and *The Letters of Katherine Mansfield,* ed. by John Middleton Murry.

McBride Co., Inc., *Adventures of a Bookseller,* by Giuseppe Orioli.

Julian Messner, Inc., *Between Two Worlds,* by John Middleton Murry.

New Directions, *Katherine Mansfield,* by Jeffrey Meyers.

Penguin Books Ltd., *The White Peacock, The Rainbow, Women in Love,* and *Kangaroo,* by D. H. Lawrence.

Martin Secker and Warburg, Ltd., *The Savage Pilgrimage: A Narrative of D. H. Lawrence,* by Catherine Carswell.

The Viking Press, Inc., *Phoenix, The Posthumous Papers,* by D. H. Lawrence, ed. by Edward McDonald; *Phoenix II,* by D. H. Lawrence, ed. by Warren Roberts & Harry T. Moore; and *Not I, But the Wind,* by Frieda Lawrence Ravagli.

Weidenfeld and Nicolson, *DHL: Novelist, Poet, Prophet,* ed. by Stephen Spender.

William and Norgate, Ltd., *Musical Chairs, or Between Two Stools,* by Cecil Gray.

The University of Wisconsin Press, *D. H. Lawrence: A Composite Biography,* Vol. 1, 2, and 3, ed. by Edward Nehls.

Further acknowledgments are made to the following periodical publications:

*John Bull,* September 17, 1921, "On Women in Love," by W. Charles Pilley.

*Everyman,* May 14, 1934, "Letter to the Editor," by Ada Lawrence Clarke.

*Harper's Magazine,* CCVI, No. 1233, contribution by Bertrand Russell.

*The D. H. Lawrence Review,* Vol. 8, No. 1, "Making Another Lawrence," by Emile Delavenay.

*New Statesman,* November 20, 1915, contribution by J. C. Squires as Solomon Eagle.

*Sphere,* October 23, 1915, contribution by Clement Shorter.

*Star,* October 22, 1915, contribution by James Douglas.

# List of Illustrations *

* All photographs listed, with the exception of the frontispiece, appear in the center of this book.

# Introduction

Stanley Hocking gave me the beginnings of this book. I met him while searching for the records of my paternal ancestors in St. Ives, Cornwall, England during the winter of 1967-1968. The search was frustrating and only moderately successful. Parish records didn't provide a complete picture, but each tiny detail uncovered led to still another, and in the process my interest sharpened. Several of my ancestors had lived near Tregerthen, in Zennor, Cornwall, during the middle of the eighteenth century. Someone suggested that I see Stanley Hocking. The Hocking family had been tenants on Tregerthen farm for several generations.

As I expected, Mr. Hocking had no knowledge of my family, and he was unable to suggest where I might look for further information. But I found that Stanley Hocking had an astonishing memory, and I was impressed with his ability to present incidents from his past. He made life on Tregerthen farm very real for me. When a second cup of tea was offered by Mrs. Hocking, I accepted gratefully. Hocking told me that he had given up Tregerthen in 1962 when he retired and moved to St. Ives. "It was a good life," he said, and then pausing, added: "I find it easier to remember little things that happened more than fifty years ago than to recall things that went on last week!" And what did he consider to be the most interesting time in his life? "I've had many," he replied, "but I'm sure it would be the time when D. H. Lawrence and his wife, Frieda, were with us."

I was a very inquisitive visitor for the next hour and a half. Mr. Hocking barely had time to answer one question before I interrupted with another. I could see that my curiosity pleased him, and he was in no hurry to change the subject. Near the end of our long talk, he asked Mrs. Hocking to fetch his Lawrence clippings and an example of Lawrence's needlework, explaining to me that he had difficulties at times with his legs—particularly when "negotiating" a staircase. Mrs. Hocking returned with a metal box filled with yellowing newspaper clippings and what appeared to be a glass-framed picture. Hocking rose stiffly from his chair. "This is a little keepsake that Lawrence gave us Hockings," he said. It was a tapestry of the phoenix on its nest of flames. "Lawrence made this," Hocking explained. "He was very often busy with a needle." I could see the work was valuable and of great importance. Hocking was aware of this too, but as he talked I realized that he regarded the keepsake more as a reminder of the past—an object he could look at when his remarkable memory wasn't enough to satisfy him. Before I left, he showed me his clippings and a school composition book in which he had written "a few notes" about Lawrence and Frieda. His material lacked organization, but the little he had recorded had been presented interestingly. He had a definite feeling for words, and I told him this. He was happy to have my confidence in a matter which obviously plagued him, though he waved my opinion aside, pausing to say: "I don't suppose I shall ever get it all down." We talked about other matters for a few minutes, and Lawrence wasn't brought up again until I was at the door thanking the Hockings for a very enjoyable afternoon. "Our little chat has brought to mind several items about Lawrence that I had forgotten," he declared as I left.

I found myself looking for books on Lawrence during my next few visits at the St. Ives Library. I took home the two volumes of *The Collected Letters of D. H. Lawrence*, edited by Harry T. Moore; Lawrence's Australian novel, *Kangaroo*; and Moore's biography, *The Intelligent Heart*. Stanley Hocking's account of Lawrence in Cornwall gave color to the Cornish material found in these books. I made notes on details that seemed to contradict some of Hocking's recollections, and I reread "The Nightmare" chapter of *Kangaroo*—Lawrence's impressions of life in wartime England during World War I. I found this chapter exciting reading after having listened to Stanley Hocking.

It was more than a month before I saw Hocking again. I had just come out of a St. Ives shop as he was passing by. "You know," he said, "I've been thinking more and more about Lawrence since you dropped in." I told him that I was delighted to hear this and expressed interest in our getting together again soon. He replied that he would be pleased if we did. "It's a pity I didn't have my tape recorder with me that day I came to see you," I said. The thought of recording our conversation didn't trouble him, though he did express some concern as to how his voice would sound coming from a machine. After being assured that he would be agreeably surprised, he looked at me and said: "Look here, lad, why don't we get together and see how our next little talk sounds on your recorder."

I had a bottle of port wine and the recorder waiting when Hocking arrived at my cottage. For more than two hours I asked questions and he answered them. In the beginning of the interview he was aware of the machine, but the wine and the informal atmosphere of the surroundings soon relaxed him. His speech rhythms seemed to erase the years for him and he was back on Tregerthen farm and Lawrence lived nearby. At times, when he was caught in a sort of trance by his own words, his reactions were those of a sixteen-year-old farm boy. I shall never forget his reply when I asked him if Lawrence liked Cornwall. "Of course he did. He could do what he wanted. He could go swimming at Wicca Pool, he could walk to St. Ives, he could take a ride in Tom Berryman's cart"—the enviable position of being an adult, as seen by a farm boy who must spend all day in the harvest fields.

The tape had run out, the bottle of port was empty, and the interview was obviously over. But we both sat on: he, lost in a world he had known so well; I, the curious listener, sorry to have that world end so soon. "What are you going to do with it?" Hocking asked as he rose stiffly from his chair. For a moment I didn't understand him, and then the significance of his question became clear to me. I told him that I wanted to publish the interview in a magazine. "It will be more than I have done," he said with a sigh. "You have my permission to do what you like with it."

I made a transcript of the interview the following week while my family and I were visiting in London, and I combed the city for more books on Lawrence. I was disappointed to find that little had been written about Lawrence's farm friends. His letters to fellow writers about his literary activities at Higher Tregerthen were faithfully recorded—so much so that I began to doubt Stanley Hocking. How could Lawrence be so prolific as a writer and become so involved with his literary associates and still find time for the Hockings? A closer look at the letters that Lawrence wrote in Cornwall and another reading of "The Nightmare" chapter of *Kangaroo* went far to restore my confidence in Hocking. What Stanley Hocking had done was to give me a rare glimpse of Lawrence: a stranger who came into the Hockings' hayfield "to be like them"; someone who enjoyed sitting, on lonely winter nights, by the old Cornish slab; a man who was completely at ease with this farm family.

I met Hocking down by the St. Ives docks shortly after my return from London. I asked him if it would be possible for us to visit again, and he declared that it "would indeed be very possible." We made arrangements to meet over the same refreshments at my cottage.

He was in fine form throughout that second recorded inter-view—relaxed and amusing. I found myself questioning him closely several times during the long session, particularly when his enthusi-asm for the days gone by led me to think that he was exaggerating. Hocking usually had a reasonable explanation at hand, and when one was not available immediately he competently produced some new pieces of information to satisfy my curiosity. He may have been only a boy of sixteen when Lawrence lived nearby, but Hocking was born with a sharp eye for detail. There was the risk that Lawrence loomed more than lifelike in his mind—I could see this as a danger during our first long talk—but Hocking had integrity and a genuine desire to get at some truth about Lawrence.

The afternoon light was waning when Hocking rose slowly from his chair. I felt it had been a most successful visit. When I came back into the parlor with his coat and hat I asked him if there were relatives or friends around Cornwall who had known Lawrence. And would they be willing to meet with me? A troubled look etched his face in the dying light. "No one who knew Lawrence the way I knew him." The man obviously didn't want me to involve his family or friends. I said no more, and he soon left with renewed good cheer.

I didn't have to wait long before I made contact with other members of the Hocking family. The opportunity presented itself a few days later when I dropped off some film at the Studio St. Ives. Stanley Hocking's name came up quite by chance in a conversation with Doreen Blandford, wife of the shop owner. Mrs. Blandford knew the Hocking family well. Kitty Rogers, daughter of William Henry Hocking, was Mrs. Blandford's friend. Yes, she could see no reason why I shouldn't meet with Mrs. Rogers, and Mrs. Blandford would call and ask. I had no more than returned to my cottage when the telephone rang and it was Kitty Rogers on the line. Mrs. Rogers had heard that I was interviewing her Uncle Stanley and would I come over the following afternoon?

Kitty Rogers and her husband lived at Hellesveor farm, on the road to Zennor, only two miles from St. Ives. Mr. Rogers worked the farm, and Mrs. Rogers had several trailers she rented to summer visitors. They both made me feel at home the moment I entered their kitchen. Mrs. Rogers felt that her uncle had more information on

Lawrence than any member of her family. "But I don't think you will get the whole story of those days until you know more about Father. Lawrence was very fond of him." Carefully, and with some fear of jeopardizing my chance of learning more about William Henry, I told her that her uncle seemed reluctant to have me meet other members of his family. "Father and Uncle Stanley never got on well," she smiled. "They never did! I don't suppose he wants to cause more trouble. That's why he doesn't have more to say about Father." Kitty Rogers knew very little about Lawrence, and she had never heard her father mention him. "Perhaps my Uncle Philip can help you," she said, "and there are other relatives you may want to meet." I told her that I was interested in seeing them all. After we had coffee and some of her hot biscuits, she brought out a photograph of William Henry—as he must have looked when Lawrence lived in Cornwall. I couldn't resist asking if I could have a copy of the photograph made at Blandford's studio, and to my great delight she had no objections. Before I left Hellesveor farm, she arranged for me to see one of her uncles, P. O. Eddy, brother of William Henry's wife.

I took a bus inland to interview Mr. Eddy. Mrs. Rogers had given me instructions and P. O. Eddy was waiting to fetch me from the bus. We walked up a lane to the Eddys' attractive home. Mrs. Eddy had out her best tea service and there were thinly-sliced sandwiches. She was hospitable and frankly curious about Americans. I had trouble understanding Mr. Eddy's Cornish accent at first, but by the time he had shown me his many trophies—trophies he had won at cattle shows—I began to feel more comfortable. We spoke of holsteins and guernseys, then a long discussion on the poor milk yield of Durham cows followed. He had known Lawrence but not well. "We would say 'hello' in passing. Those two, William Henry and Lawrence, were very often together." P. O. Eddy had a keen sense of humor, and he was filled with stories about the days when William Henry kept the vicinity of Tregerthen in an uproar with practical jokes. Mr. Eddy speculated at length on how different William Henry's life would have been with an education. When P. O. Eddy walked me back to my bus, he declared: "You know a bit about farming, lad. That's unusual in this day and age. I wouldn't have talked like I did if you hadn't experienced life on a farm."

My knowledge of farming was of little help to me when I met with Kitty Roger's youngest brother, John Hocking. "If you want to know what William Henry was like," P. O. Eddy had said, "then go look at John. Those two are the same." John Hocking did resemble his father. Remarkably so. He was clearing out a stable as I entered his yard one cold January afternoon. I felt I had just stepped into the photograph Mrs. Rogers had given me. "I don't know why you've come," said John Hocking, "and I can't see what good it will do." I told him I didn't know either, but I was interested in Lawrence and his father. Hocking took me into his house. His wife was away shopping in St. Ives. "A man called Edward Nehls was once here asking us questions," he said. "We never did learn what he did with the details." Hocking then produced a holograph of an untitled poem Lawrence had written for William Henry. The poem disappeared before I had time to examine it closely. I asked John Hocking several questions about his father and Lawrence. He answered them as best he could, but when I turned on my recorder to dictate a point he had made, Hocking became alarmed. I explained that I wanted to use the machine to take notes. I could see that he much preferred me to use an older invention—the pencil I had with me. The interview, if it could be called that, was short and unproductive. He took me into his shed on our way out and showed me an old dresser that once was Lawrence's. I left with the feeling that John Hocking was pleased to have my visit over.

"Don't mind John," Kitty Rogers assured me later that week. "There's a rumor going that you're up to no good." Mrs. Rogers was amused. A member of the Hocking family had voiced an opinion of my frequent jaunts around St. Ives and in the vicinity of Tregerthen. I had been referred to as "that wretched American." This stung me more than I wanted to admit, but thinking it over I could see that I was really no different than the few brash journalists who had questioned the Hockings in the past. Perhaps I was "out to get information for my own gain"—an expression I had heard from several suspicious Cornishmen in St. Ives.

My feelings of guilt increased when I met with Mary Hocking, Stanley and William Henry's sister, at the Rogers' home. Mary Hocking sat quietly at the kitchen table while the others talked. She seemed so sad and withdrawn. But a lovely expression came over her face when I brought up Lawrence's name. "She may have nothing to say," Mrs. Rogers had warned me earlier. For more than ten minutes the elderly Miss Hocking spoke of that time when Lawrence and Frieda were neighbors. Then, suddenly, as if she had misplaced the handkerchief she held in her hand, she stopped talking, and tears appeared in her eyes. "They are all gone," she said in a broken voice. "Tregerthen is no more." She then rose from the table and went into the parlor to be alone with her thoughts and the past.

Norman Levine, the Canadian poet, lived at the head of our street. Levine had married an English girl and they had been in St. Ives for several years. I brought up the Hockings one evening while visiting. "I don't know much about the Hockings," Levine admitted, "but if you really want to hear Lawrence stories, you should see 'Pop' Short—he's fun."

Ivor Short, the son of the old sea captain who had leased Higher Tregerthen to Lawrence, was one of the liveliest men I have ever met. He was well into his eighties then, and calling on him was like going to a noisy saloon. People were constantly running in and out of his home near the St. Ives wharf. I visited him several times during my stay in Cornwall, and on one occasion Short hired a car to show me the home he had bought for his daughter in nearby Lelant. Ivor Short blamed the farmers who lived near Lawrence for the "war madness" and there was "nothing but gossip going on out there all the time." He was very fond of Frieda. He recalled the time when his brother was inoculated with a contaminated needle—"my brother was never any good after that," Short declared. But it was Frieda who wrote to her family in Germany to have some new medicine shipped to England for his brother. "She was one of the kindest women I ever knew," said Short. The William Henry-Lawrence friendship completely mystified him. "I don't know how it came about or why. They had nothing in common."

Kitty Rogers arranged for me to meet with still another Hocking, her brother Henry. I spent an afternoon with him at his Trevega farmhouse—the farm William Henry had operated after leaving Tregerthen. Henry H. Hocking and I sat talking in his dining room while his young son crawled under the chairs and upon our laps. At the end of our long talk, Hocking showed me the desk Lawrence had used at Higher Tregerthen—an old maple piece prominently displayed in Hocking's parlor. "I've told you everything I know," he said as I departed. "I hope you will write it the way it was."

I had recorded several reels of tape before I saw the first hints of spring in St. Ives and on the Zennor footpaths. My time in Cornwall was coming to an end. Our family passports had been validated for only a six-month stay in England, and we had made plans to spend the summer in Ireland. It was necessary to conclude my Lawrence activities, and when the weather turned sunny and warm Stanley Hocking and I spent several hours one day at Tregerthen farm and Higher Tregerthen. Evan and Doreen Blandford accompanied us with photographic equipment. Stanley Hocking pointed out the various settings where the many dramas took place. "I can see Lawrence crossing that little field now," said Hocking. "It seems only yesterday that Lawrence and Frieda were with us." Then Stanley Hocking shook his head. "It all happened fifty years ago."

Lawrence At Tregerthen

# I

A man and woman were walking along a footpath at Treger-then. It was a late afternoon in early March of 1916. The couple saw a Cornishman in a nearby field and they stopped to talk. The young farmer was Stanley Hocking.

"At first sight," said Hocking, "they seemed to be a rather odd-looking pair, if you will. Lawrence had a ginger-colored beard, and he was dressed in a brown corduroy suit. He was wearing a slouch hat. Frieda was a very good-looking lady, fair and blonde, and above all things, she was wearing red stockings. They said good evening very nicely. They asked me if I lived at the farm. I told them I was born there, and my grandfather and his grandfather before him. 'Oh yes, that's interesting,' Lawrence said. 'We like this part of the world, and we think it would be an awfully nice place to stay. We'd like to live somewhere near here.' He said they were staying in Zennor, at the Tinners Arms, but it would be for only a week or two. 'Do you know of any vacant cottages around here?' Lawrence asked. 'Oh yes, those cottages over there are all vacant at this moment,' I told him. They were Higher Tregerthen. 'They look rather nice,' Lawrence said. 'Do you think I could get hold of one?' I told him the name of the owner, and if he wanted to go see him there wouldn't be any harm done. The owner was Captain Short, an old sea captain who lived in St. Ives. 'Good,' said Lawrence. 'I'll see him tomorrow.' "

The Lawrences liked Captain Short and his wife Lucy. Short had been retired from the sea for six years, but he still wore a captain's uniform. The local fishermen would always go to Captain Short when they were in need of advice. One St. Ives fisherman recalled that he had his nets taken away from him in a legal wrangle, and it was Short who had engaged a solicitor for him to make sure that compensation was paid. The old sea captain and his son, Ivor, showed the couple the Zennor property, and the Lawrences were delighted.

"Lawrence and Frieda called at the farm a few days after-wards," said Stanley Hocking. "Mother and I were there. They told us that they had succeeded in renting a cottage at Higher Tregerthen for five pounds a year. Mind you, it was only a small place and unfurnished. Lawrence said they were going to get a few sticks of furniture together and go there to live. He said they hoped that they could get their few necessities of life from the farm. Mother said they could. So within a few days they got some secondhand furniture in St. Ives and moved into the cottage."

Higher Tregerthen was once five cottages occupied by farm laborers and their families. Long before Lawrence went there to live, the farm workers had moved in and out of the cottages frequently. "It was a place for dubious characters," said Stanley Hocking. "I suppose the people who lived there were married, but they never stayed for long." Author Guy Thorne, known as Ranger Gull, caused much local gossip and criticism. Thorne leased the larger of the two buildings at Higher Tregerthen, had three of the cottages knocked into one, made a tower room out of an end bedroom upstairs, and never came back. "He is a scamp," Lawrence told the Hockings after hearing the story from Captain Short.

The two-roomed cottage that Lawrence and Frieda leased was in the smaller building. The narrow lane, from Eagles Nest on the St. Ives road, went past the front door of Lawrence's new home and on to nearby Tregerthen farm. Beyond the farm, the sea with an occasional convoy of ships. Lawrence loved the surroundings, and he wanted his friends, John Middleton Murry and Katherine Mansfield, to lease the tower cottage. He hoped another friend, Philip Heseltine, would be exempted from serving in the military and would stay at Higher Tregerthen too. Perhaps Heseltine could live with the Murrys, Lawrence wrote them, and they could all eat in the dining room of the tower part—an arrangement the Murrys found less than agreeable.

Philip Heseltine had just spent several weeks with the Lawrences in J. D. Beresford's farmhouse in Padstow, Cornwall. Heseltine now had other ideas. He was not returning to Lawrence. He was taking a small studio attic in London. Relations with Lawrence were impossible. The man was insane, claimed Heseltine, and had caused trouble when interfering in his life by trying to arrange matrimony.

Lawrence persisted in coaxing the Murrys to leave Bandol, in the south of France, and come to Cornwall. His three letters to them, all within a week, took on the tone of an accomplished fact. He was sure that they would live for a long time at Higher Tregerthen, and that the war would soon be over. "Let it be agreed for ever," Lawrence wrote Murry, "I am *Blutbruder:* a *Blutbruderschaft* between us all. Tell K. *not* to be so queasy."[1] But Katherine Mansfield had once stayed in Cornwall, and she had seen a Cornish woman torturing a cat. She had decided that Cornish women were cruel. In a poem, she wrote: "And such eyes!/Stupid, shifty, small and sly/Peeping through a slit of sty."[2] The decision to leave their Villa Pauline was difficult for the Murrys, but Lawrence's demands could not be denied. Katherine Mansfield wept on the day she and Murry left Bandol for Cornwall.

The Lawrences were busy settling into their small cottage while waiting for the Murrys. So little was needed to make the two rooms comfortable and attractive. Lawrence, happy to make the smallest household task a kind of religious ritual, did his own carpentry.

"Lawrence could turn his hand to anything," said Stanley Hocking. "I remember seeing a dresser he made, and I can see the walls he painted. Pale pink walls, and the cupboards bright blue. He could cook too. He was a bit effeminate, and he did some embroidery work. There were a few paintings that Lawrence did on odd scraps of paper, pinned up near the scullery. But I don't think Lawrence or Frieda attached any importance to them. They were very roughly done, hanging with several little bits of Lawrence's crochet work. He started doing the phoenix he gave us before he left Cornwall. But he hadn't finished it. I remember him saying to me before he went away: 'I am taking the phoenix rising from the flames to be my motto. For out of the dead ashes of my past I'm going to make a living future for myself.' Well, he took the phoenix back to London with him, and when he finished it, he sent it down to us. He wanted us to have it. For a while it was lying, as you might say, untouched. Finally, a friend of my mother's took it in hand and got it framed. That's how it's been ever since. To use an old Cornish saying: Lawrence 'could wash, mend, bake and sew'—a saying of my mother's."

"I saw him knitting once when I went over to visit him with my father and mother," said Ivor Short. "If I recall correctly, he was knitting a jumper. It was a hobby of his. It gave him something to do."

The Hockings at Tregerthen farm were very sociable and curious about this man with the ginger-colored beard and his German wife. Lawrence was cordial, though careful when answering their questions. Tregerthen farm was close to his cottage, just across a small field where the lambs skipped into the air "like little explosions."[3] The widowed Mrs. Hocking had a warmth which was disarming, and her handsome son, William Henry, who was Lawrence's age, soon sparked conversation. Lawrence was fascinated by these people who possessed an endless curiosity about the world, and who had an intense interest in what was right.

Lawrence was at the St. Ives railway station to meet the Murrys. This should have been a happy reunion, but the Murrys' lack of enthusiasm was thinly disguised. A cold wind was blowing up St. Ives Bay from the Bristol Channel and the all-day complaining gulls were circling in a gray sky. They hired a cart to take them all to Higher Tregerthen, and when Katherine Mansfield and Middleton Murry looked down at the alien moors from Eagles Nest, they knew they had made a mistake. The Murrys thought Tregerthen cold and dismal. But for Lawrence's benefit they tried to keep up some pretense of being impressed and happy.

In Frieda Lawrence's book, *Not I, But the Wind*, she recalled: "I see Katherine Mansfield arriving, sitting on a cart high up on all the goods and chattels, coming down the lane to Tregerthen. Like an emigrant, Katherine looked. I loved her little jackets, chiefly the one that was black and gold like bees."[4] Later, in their room at the Tinners Arms, where they were to stay until they were ready to settle into the tower cottage, Katherine Mansfield confessed to Murry that she hated the place.

Lawrence and Frieda took the Murrys into St. Ives to meet their new landlord and to shop for cheap furniture. At Benny's salesroom they found a wide selection of old but sound things left by St. Ives fishermen who had bought new furnishings. These purchases were taken back to Higher Tregerthen in a shaky cart that rattled down the lane. Then a flurry of activity broke out as they repaired and arranged all the bargains they had bought. Murry painted his chairs black to match his mood while Katherine Mansfield looked on approvingly. "Look at the funeral procession of chairs," she said.[5] They were unaware that these chairs were omens for the days to follow.

## II

Lawrence and Frieda first met John Middleton Murry and Katherine Mansfield during the summer of 1913 when the Lawrences visited the Murrys' three-roomed flat at 57 Chancery Lane in London. The flat was also the business office for *The Blue Review*, a magazine the Murrys were then coediting. Lawrence had sent his story, "The Soiled Rose," to the Murrys' earlier magazine, *Rhythm*. The Lawrences arrived on a sunny day, and they all rode on a bus to Soho for lunch. Frieda warmed to the young couple when she caught them making faces at one another, and Lawrence mistakenly thought the Murrys were wealthy and important. "We liked one another," Murry recalled, "and when it emerged, as it quickly did, that Katherine and I were not married, and that Katherine like Frieda was waiting to be divorced, it began to appear . . . that we were made for one another."[1]

John Middleton Murry, who was ten months younger than Katherine Mansfield, was born in 1889, in a South London suburb, of poor middle-class parents. His father was a clerk in the War Office and a petty tyrant at home. After a repressive childhood, Murry went to Oxford on a scholarship. He worked as a journalist in London and met Katherine in December 1911. Katherine Mansfield, the pseudonym of Kathleen Beauchamp, was a third-generation New Zealander—the daughter of merchant Sir Harold Beauchamp. She received her education in her own country and later studied in London. Murry and Katherine fell in love and soon embarked on literary careers, but they were unable to marry until 1918 when Katherine finally succeeded in divorcing the musician George Bowden. When Murry met the Lawrences, he was a handsome, wide-mouthed, energetic young man who wore his hair in a long bang that came down above his right eye. Katherine Mansfield was a curiously attractive person, Slav in appearance, and very determined in her actions. She had dark eyes, was not tall, wore her hair in an unfashionable bob, and she, like Murry, had bangs.

Lawrence invited the Murrys to see him on the Kentish coast

where he and Frieda had gone to stay after the London visit. The Murrys were unable to finance the trip, and when Lawrence heard of their plight he wrote Murry a letter reproaching him for not asking for a loan. When the Murrys did visit, along with Murry's friend Gordon Campbell, they all bathed together in the sea at dusk and made a banquet of tomatoes and beefsteaks. Lawrence gave the Murrys a copy of his *Sons and Lovers* and they were terribly impressed. "Lawrence was a really new experience," Murry wrote. "He seemed straightway to be taking charge of my affairs, unravelling the tangle."[2] Lawrence had no sympathy for Murry's current problems with the dying *Blue Review* and insisted that Murry and Katherine come and live beside him in Italy that winter. Murry felt it would be impossible to break away then, and if he should it would mean having to live on Katherine's allowance. But this didn't discourage Lawrence. He could get them a nice apartment in Italy with a big garden for so little. They must try to come. Though Lawrence was unable to work his will upon them at that time, he did kindle in Murry's mind the idea of breaking away from England and going to Paris for a short stay.

The visits together were resumed immediately upon the Lawrences' return to England the following summer. Katherine Mansfield, Murry, and Gordon Campbell were witnesses when Lawrence and Frieda were married, on July 13, 1914, at a registry office in London. Katherine was deeply moved when Frieda gave her wedding ring to her—the ring from Frieda's previous marriage to Professor Ernest Weekley. Katherine Mansfield wore the ring all her life and it was on her finger when she was buried at Fontainebleau.

The Lawrences were staying at the Gordon Campbells, and the Campbells' tiny parlor became a place for friends and literary acquaintances to meet. This was the first time that Murry had been with Lawrence long enough to study his new friend closely, and Murry was left confused. He was unable to fathom Lawrence's moods and he didn't understand what Lawrence was trying to convey in their relationship. Lawrence's *Sons and Lovers* had been discovered by Freudian psychoanalysts who felt the book exemplified some of Freud's main themes. Lawrence was called upon more than once to discuss the doctrine while Murry was present. Murry couldn't understand why sex was being taken so seriously. He claimed that it had been no problem in his life. But Lawrence felt that both Murry and Katherine took sex too lightly. He disliked their flippancy. "If we were abnormal," Murry observed, "our abnormality lay in the fact that we were unusually happy as lovers, and we felt that, in this one thing, we were a good deal happier than Lawrence and Frieda."[3]

Flaws in their relationship soon appeared, but still the four met. Their serious talks together never seemed to reach the expected high level of meaningfulness, and they were often left with feelings of frustration and dissatisfaction. Recalling this time, in his last letter to Murry, on May 20, 1929, Lawrence wrote: "By pretending a bit, we had some jolly times, in the past. But we all had to pretend a bit—and we could none of us keep it up."[4] There was a closeness, claimed Murry, and some understanding. They were conscious of the uncertain world around them, and it was this uncertainty which made them hopeful of their friendship. But they did have to ignore the differences that sealed them from each other in their intimate lives. "What glimpses they had of ours," wrote Murry, "and we of theirs, were alike incomprehensible. Nor, I think, could it have been otherwise."[5]

Two things were on Lawrence's mind during the early fall of 1914: one was the war, and the other was the struggle he was having with Frieda. Lawrence knew that the war would make it impossible for him to return to Italy as he had planned, and he soon found a cottage near Chesham, in Buckinghamshire, for the remainder of the year. The Murrys were invited for a weekend, and since they had to find quarters for themselves Lawrence induced them to come live nearby. It was here that the Murrys first experienced the desperate quarrels that raged between Lawrence and Frieda. Murry and Katherine Mansfield, like all of Lawrence's friends, were dragged into the fray. The battling couple seemed to take pleasure in involving others. Lawrence had grown a beard and he appeared to be ill. It was not the best of times. Murry recalled an occasion when Lawrence visited him. It was a black night and Lawrence had walked the three miles between their houses. He came in and said nothing. He sat in a rocking chair by the stove and began rocking and moaning. Murry guessed that Lawrence and Frieda had had another quarrel. But there had been no fight. It turned out that the horror of the world at war had been too much for Lawrence to bear and he had come to be near his friend. Another incident was recalled by Murry. He and Katherine had dined with the Lawrences one evening. The dishes had been washed and pleasant conversation reigned. Then there was some mention of the three children Frieda had left when she went to live with Lawrence. Frieda burst into tears and Lawrence went white. He had had enough of the woman and she must leave him forever. He would give her a share of their money—more than her rightful share. He counted sixteen sovereigns in the presence of the Murrys and threw the gold coins on the table. Frieda stood at the door, crying. She had on her coat and hat but was at a loss as to where she would go. Murry, strangely enough, sided with Lawrence at the time of the quarrel.

Among the visitors in Buckinghamshire that fall was Samuel Solomonovich Koteliansky. "Kot," as he was known, was the man to whom Lawrence wrote more frequently than to any other person. Lawrence had met him on a walking tour of the Lake Country at the outbreak of the war. Koteliansky had come to England only a few years before on a scholarship from the University of Kiev to do research in economics. He had been under suspicion in his own country for his radical views and had elected to stay on in England. With various British authors, including Lawrence, Koteliansky translated more than thirty Russian works into English. Koteliansky liked Lawrence immensely, but the swarthy Russian with the fiery black glances could never warm to Frieda. Nor she to him. In *Lorenzo in Taos*, Mabel Dodge Luhan revealed Frieda's feelings for Koteliansky. He was the enemy, Frieda's enemy. Kot felt that she wasn't good enough for Lawrence; that she didn't do enough for her husband. Frieda claimed that Koteliansky wanted to separate them. "Everyone thinks Lawrence is so wonderful." Frieda reportedly told Mrs. Luhan. "Well, I'd like to see him (Kot) live with Lawrence a month—a week! He might be surprised."[6]

"Koteliansky was, at this period, by far Katherine's most understandable friend," recalled Middleton Murry.[7] There was more than friendship involved here and Murry was aware of it. He knew about Katherine's destructive sexual encounters, her lesbianism, and her frequent affairs with men, including painter Mark Gertler, but Murry preferred to overlook these adventures. Though they were able to survive numerous disasters as a couple, many of Mansfield's friends felt that Murry was afraid of life and lacked the vitality to make his and Katherine's relationship a success. From the beginning of their marriage, Katherine took the dominant role and he comfortably became the submissive partner. The Lawrences' sympathies were with Murry while Koteliansky stood by Katherine—Koteliansky delighting in her escapades.

A circle of friends gathered that fall and early winter in Chesham. Novelist Gilbert Cannan had married actress Mary Ansell and they lived in nearby Cholesbury with their house guest Mark Gertler.

Gertler had come to recover from a long period of overwork and socializing in London. That Christmas the Cannans celebrated with a dinner party of roast suckling pig, which no one knew how to carve, and there was too much to drink. In the midst of charades, Koteliansky got the idea of a play within a play. Sensing trouble in the Murrys' relationship, and being in love with Katherine, Koteliansky called for a dramatization with Gertler to act the role of Murry's successor. Murry and Katherine played their parts convincingly until the third act, which was supposed to end with a reconciliation. It was then that Katherine Mansfield refused to follow the script—she insisted on staying with Gertler. Lawrence exploded and lashed out at Murry for exposing himself in such a way. Didn't he know? Was he blind?

These were the people that Lawrence had recruited for the dream of an ideal community. Rananim was the name, from one of Koteliansky's Hebrew songs. Lawrence wanted a dozen or more people to accompany him to a remote spot on earth where they could form a moneyless colony and practice a sort of communism for the necessities of life and realize decency and goodness. In *Not I, But the Wind*, Frieda Lawrence recalled: "Katherine and Lawrence and Murry had invented a place, a wonderful place where we were all going to live in complete bliss; Rananim it was called. Lawrence thought of the new spirit of the life we would try to live there. Murry thought of the ship, and its equipment, that would take us to our island of Rananim. Katherine saw all the colored bundles that we would have to take."[8] But when Katherine Mansfield studied maps and gathered practical information about the islands and the remote areas where they might go, she became doubtful and questioned Lawrence closely. He fell silent and said no more.

Lawrence and Frieda found the house at Chesham too cramped and uncomfortable, and when author and editor Wilfred Meynell and his family offered one of the Meynell cottages on an eighty acre tract of land in Sussex, the Lawrences left Chesham, happy to be on the move again. But the Murrys were not forgotten. The scenario performed at the Cannans' had become all too real for Middleton Murry. Katherine was going to leave him; she was in love with French novelist Francis Carco whom the Murrys had met in Paris the previous winter. Lawrence asked Murry to Sussex when Katherine Mansfield left for France and his friend arrived cold and wet and ill with influenza. Lawrence put Murry to bed and kept him there for two days. But on the third day Lawrence opened fire. He insisted that

Murry's friendship with Gordon Campbell was the cause for the split—the two had ignored Katherine when they talked and Murry had no one but himself to blame. This was enough to convince Murry that he would have no more to do with Campbell. "That it might have been so," Murry admitted, "I could not deny; for it needed a far more certain knowledge of myself than I possessed to deny it pointblank." Lawrence also spoke at length on the need for revolution: nationalization of land, industry, railways—a doctrine similar to the one he was offering in letters to Bertrand Russell. Murry, who had already lost Katherine and Campbell, was quick to agree with everything Lawrence said. "I was like a woman," Murry wrote in *Between Two Worlds*, "instinctively humouring her husband by accepting his arguments and principles, although in fact they are quite indifferent to her; but, unlike a woman, I was uneasy about it, and sought desperately to convince myself that I really did agree."[9] The visit ended when Murry received a telegram from Katherine Mansfield. She was returning to him and London. Murry hurriedly left Sussex to meet her train.

In early August, 1915, the Lawrences moved to a small flat at 1 Byron Villas in Hampstead. Frieda needed to be near her children. The Murrys were together again in London and Lawrence was quick to visit them. They all talked about breaking away from England and made plans for a series of pamphlets. Since hopes for a Rananim were temporarily postponed, their desires to do something meaningful materialized in the announcement of a pamphlet to be called *The Signature*. Koteliansky had found an inexpensive printer and the goal was to get £30 in subscriptions—enough for six issues. But the idea soon expanded. They rented a room off Red Lion Square, to be used as an editorial office and a meeting place. Only £15 in subscriptions was realized from leaflets and after the third number *The Signature* expired. Lawrence contributed his essay "The Crown," Katherine Mansfield, as "Matilda Berry," was represented with two of her stories, and Murry wrote an autobiographical piece called "There Was a Little Man."

Then word came that Katherine Mansfield's brother had been killed on the battlefield in France. Katherine felt a need to get away from England for a time. She and Murry decided to stay in the south of France. The Lawrences were making plans to leave too. For Florida. They had had enough of the war and the mob spirit of London. The sailing date was set for the 20th of December, from Glasgow to Key West, but a week before departure Lawrence was told that they couldn't get passports. Within a day or two he had made up his mind to go to Cornwall.

The intense friendship which developed between Lawrence and Murry was doomed to fail, though in the beginning it seemed to be one of permanence. To Frieda, Katherine was the younger sister who carried messages to Frieda's children in Hampstead—Monty, Barby and Elsa. Lawrence wanted a blood bond with Murry: an ideal friendship which knew no boundaries. But temperamental outbursts and criticisms from Lawrence provoked Murry. Once, after Katherine Mansfield's early death at the age of thirty-five, and with Lawrence in America, Frieda met Murry in London. She had quarreled bitterly with Lawrence and had left him. She had had enough of his black, ugly moods. Frieda and Murry decided to go to Germany together and on the way they declared their love to each other. Frieda wanted them to stay together in Freiburg for a few days, but the idea of sleeping together was too much for Murry. He was worn out by Katherine Mansfield's long illness. "No, my darling, I mustn't let Lorenzo down—I can't." According to Murry, it was only after Lawrence's death, when Murry visited Lawrence's grave in Vence, that he met Frieda and they became lovers. In Murry's *Journal*, 1954, he wrote: "With her, and with her for the first time in my life, I knew what fulfillment in love really meant."[10]

Murry's critical biography of Lawrence, *Son of Woman*, 1931, was widely criticized for creating an erroneous picture of the man. Murry defended Lawrence from several vicious death notices in English papers, but as he began to brood over their relationship Murry produced a book that damaged Lawrence's reputation. People who saw Lawrence differently were quick to point out inaccuracies. The major fault found with *Son of Woman* was that the book showed that Lawrence was a self-tortured man and neglected to mention the other side of his nature. The Lawrence-Murry quarrel continued long after Lawrence's death, finding new roots in reviews of *Son of Woman* and accounts of Lawrence which refuted Murry's claim. Ada Lawrence Clarke, Lawrence's younger sister, in a letter to the editor of *Everyman*, May 14, 1934, wrote that Murry would someday regret having published the book. She felt it revealed Murry as unworthy of the friendship he once had with her brother. Mrs. Clarke insisted that if Lawrence had been alive, Murry would never had found the courage to write the things he did. "For Lawrence was the soul of honour and truth, and sentimental hypocrisy he couldn't tolerate." She said that

Lawrence had told her that he thought it was horrible the way Murry exploited the memory of Katherine Mansfield. Ada Clarke accused Murry of overlooking Lawrence's "marvelous simplicity" with working-class people—never making them feel uneasy or inferior, and how kind he had been as a brother.[11]

It was the spring of 1916, and Lawrence's hope of founding a new colony seemed within reach. It was Rananim come true that heightened Lawrence's enthusiasm for Zennor. The Murrys had finally come to share in his dream. The war couldn't go on forever. Higher Tregerthen huddled by the sea was the place to begin.

### III

Before the Murrys were completely settled in the tower part at Higher Tregerthen, a policeman from St. Ives came with a warrant to arrest Murry for not joining the army. Murry produced a rejection certificate from the Officers Training Corps, but the policeman doubted if such a rejection was legal. After Murry explained his position carefully and Katherine Mansfield tried to assure the official that all was well, the policeman went back up the lane only partly convinced that Murry was telling the truth.

The incident left Lawrence with doubts about his own future. "I suppose they will make a clerk out of me," he told the Hockings when he came to the farm for his milk. But his unsettled feelings for the days ahead didn't slow his writing. Lawrence began a new novel as the gorse turned yellow and the early May winds rose from the misty sea. The book was *Women in Love.* "But already it is beyond all hope of ever being published, because of the things it says," Lawrence wrote Barbara Low. "And more than that it is beyond all possibility even to offer it to a world, a putrescent mankind like ours."[1] Lawrence had been feeling ill for days and hinted that it might explain the tone of his letter. The world had become too much for him. Somehow he and Murry must carry on at Higher Tregerthen until they were forced to take part in the war.

Katherine Mansfield, in a letter to Koteliansky, on May 11,

1916, explained that she hadn't written earlier because everything had been so unsettled. She was being left alone too much at Tregerthen. It wasn't a nice place. "It may all be over next month; in fact, it will be. I don't belong to anybody here." Mansfield reported that she and Frieda weren't speaking to each other. The rift had developed because Katherine couldn't tolerate the situation between Lawrence and Frieda. "I don't know which disgusts me worse. When they are very loving and playing with each other or when they are roaring at each other and he is pulling out Frieda's hair and saying 'I'll cut your bloody throat, you bitch' and Frieda is running up and down the road screaming for 'Jack' to save her." Katherine Mansfield claimed that Lawrence was no longer healthy and had gone slightly mad. "If he is contradicted about *anything* he gets into a frenzy, quite beside himself and it goes on until he is so exhausted that he cannot stand and has to go to bed and stay there until he has recovered."[2]

Stanley Hocking remembered Middleton Murry and Katherine Mansfield. "They were taking the tower part at Higher Tregerthen because they wanted to live next to the Lawrences. But they stayed for a very short time. They didn't like it at Tregerthen. The Murrys were always complaining that the place was wild, cold, and uninhabited. They didn't like the roughness of the countryside. So they packed up and went to live on the Falmouth side of the coast." Hocking didn't recall the quarrels, and after reading Mansfield's letter to Koteliansky, Hocking declared: "I don't believe it. They wouldn't have dared to print this letter if Lawrence had been living. Dead men can't hear and they don't talk. Lawrence and Frieda had their little tiffs, but I don't think they quarreled as violently as that." Hocking's sister, Mary, remembered it differently. "They fought like cats and dogs. I know, because I heard them."

Ivor Short had another impression of that time. "I first met Lawrence and Frieda when they rented the cottage in Zennor. I used to take Father and Mother over to see them with the pony and jingle cart. The Murrys stayed in the tower for a while. They were a happy crowd—there was no boozing and that sort of thing. They weren't that type at all. And Frieda was very fond of D. H. They got on very well together. I remember Lawrence would refer to her as 'my dear Frieda.' I have heard so much of this backchat about them. They had a rough time here."

Murry recalled an evening when he and Katherine Mansfield were sitting by the fire in the long room of the tower cottage when suddenly a shriek. Frieda rushed in crying: "He'll kill me!" Lawrence followed, pale and in a frenzy. He chased Frieda several times around a table, shouting: "I'll kill her, I'll kill her!" Chairs were overturned, and Murry barely managed to save a lamp. "Katherine sat still in a corner, indifferent, inexpressibly weary." Murry wrote in *Between Two Worlds*: "I was terrified. That he would have killed her, I made no doubt; and yet, for some strange reason, I had no impulse to intervene." Then suddenly, Lawrence dropped into a chair by the fire, his fury spent. They were all silent. Frieda went back to their cottage. "The three of us sat on without stirring—each in our different way, utterly exhausted." After a time Lawrence rose, pale and shaky, and said good night. The episode was over. But what bewildered the Murrys even more than this outburst was what they found when they visited the Lawrences the next morning. The two were "sitting side by side, to all appearance blissfully happy, while Lawrence trimmed a hat for Frieda."[3]

The table-chasing row was only one of many eruptions at Tregerthen. According to Murry, these usually came about from some ordinary occurrence. Frieda would contradict Lawrence and he would explode. Murry remembered one recurring argument. Frieda would "defend one of Lawrence's discarded prophets—Shelley, for example, or Nietzsche—" and she would be too sweet and reasonable. Lawrence would attack. "What do you know about Shelley? What do *you* care? If you *dare* to say another word about Shelley, I'll—," then a threat and his air of rightful indignation.[4] Murry claimed that Frieda knew the lay of the land of Lawrence's sympathies at any given moment. But still she persisted in holding her own, and against him.

Recalling this time in Cornwall, Frieda remembered "days of complete harmony between the Murrys and us. Katherine coming to our cottage so thrilled at my foxgloves, tall in the small window seat. Since then whenever I see foxgloves I must think of Katherine." And Frieda and Katherine would frequently walk to Zennor village with Katherine Mansfield stamping her feet at the high wind she hated so much, and later the two would sit talking like "two Indian braves." Then one day they all went out on the sea in a boat, and Frieda was moved when they sang "Row, row, row your boat/Gently down the stream"—Frieda finding something "strangely significant" in the words, and Lawrence's rage because "I was so bad at keeping my part of the song going."[5]

Brigit Patmore, who first met Lawrence and Frieda in London

during World War I, felt that the quarrels were never serious. Patmore suggested that the rows were aggravated by the presence of Lawrence's literary friends. But once caught in the crossfire of crockery and pots, or witnessing one of Lawrence's verbal whippings, friends found it difficult to take such performances lightly or to think of the quarrels as being therapeutic. Just under the surface an unalterable bond did exist, and perhaps it was this that kept the Lawrences together to the end.

Mabel Dodge Luhan, who knew the Lawrences in New Mexico, gave her readers this picture of Frieda: "I saw the big voluptuous woman standing naked in the dim stone room where we dressed and undressed, and there were often great black and blue bruises on her blond flesh." Then one morning Luhan found Frieda in tears. When asked what was wrong, Frieda cried: "He tears me to pieces. Last night he was so loving and so tender with me, and this morning he hates me." Such a statement came as no surprise to Mabel Luhan. She and others had been present when Lawrence shouted at Frieda: "You sniffing bitch, stop your smoking." And when Frieda asked why she should, Lawrence was enraged. "Take that dirty cigarette out of your mouth! And stop sticking out that fat belly of yours!" But Frieda wasn't defeated easily; she was quick to counterattack. "You better stop that talk or I'll tell about *your* things."[6] Lawrence jumped to his feet and swung at Frieda's head. She ducked and ran from the room. The onlookers were shocked, and their discomfiture became astonishment when they saw Lawrence and Frieda a few minutes later walking in the moonlight, arm in arm like lovers.

"I do think a woman must yield some sort of precedence to a man," Lawrence wrote Katherine Mansfield in 1918. "I can't help it, I believe this. Frieda doesn't. Hence our fight."[7] And once when confronting Frieda, Lawrence pressed her against a wall with his hands on her throat and insisted that he was her master. Frieda's reply that he could be her master as much as he liked, that it made no difference to her, surprised him so that he dropped his hands. A fight to the death was how Lawrence saw marriage, and Frieda's opposition to his wish for dominance led them close to the breaking point on more than one occasion. When really stung by his unreasonableness, she could resist with all her stout stubbornness. Their brawls were sometimes hideously petty; sometimes grand. She would rile him by smoking too much, eating too many cakes, having her hair cropped, and taking an opposite line of thought. Frieda once complained to Edward

Garnett that Lawrence "always wants to treat women like the chicken we had the other day, take its guts out and pluck its feathers sitting over a pail."[8]

Catherine Carswell's *The Savage Pilgrimage,* largely a personal narrative, revealed Lawrence as a man of immense energy, quick to fly into rages over the smallest things, and courageous. A hero who repudiated heroism. And Frieda was to Lawrence "a buffeting and a laughing breeze, a healing rain or a maddening tempest of stupidity, a cheering sun or a stroke of indiscriminating lightning."[9] Much of Carswell's book was a fence-mending reply to Murry's *Son of Woman,* but both she and Murry produced similar versions when reporting the continuous rows at Higher Tregerthen.

More than once in 1916, Frieda felt that Lawrence was mad. An incident in which she nearly brained him with a stone dinner plate showed that both were unpredictable. Lawrence was washing dishes in the scullery and singing a roundelay—he and Frieda had just concluded a bitter argument. Frieda came in from the living room carrying the stone dinner plate. The song Lawrence was singing "so wrought upon her," Carswell wrote, "that her wrath boiled up afresh. Down on the singer's head she brought the dinner plate." The plate could have injured Lawrence seriously. "But he was as far from bearing Frieda a grudge as from turning the other cheek. 'That was like a woman!' said he, turning on her viciously, but on this occasion too much astonished to strike back. 'No man could have done such a thing when the quarrel was over, and from behind too!' Then Lawrence added: 'But you *are* a woman.' "[10]

Louis Untermeyer, who first met the Lawrences in Italy and later in London, found Frieda "an almost theatrical contrast to her husband." Her solidness and good health made her "the earth-mother Lawrence was always seeking and escaping, but to which he always returned." Frieda took pride in her role and her family and she was quick to let one know that she was a von Richthofen and her husband was only a commoner. She wouldn't be pitied for the difficult days she and Lawrence shared in Cornwall "when they lived," wrote Untermeyer, "servantless and unfriended, in a flimsy shack on the coast of England." She never did the menial chores about the house. That was her spouse's task. "Lawrence scrubbed the floor. He loved it."[11]

Emma Maria Frieda Johanna von Richthofen was born in 1879, the second of three daughters of Baron and Baronin Friedrich von Richthofen of Germany. Her father had begun his career in the military and later served as an official in the civil service. Frieda grew up outside Metz and knew the Germany of Bismarck and the Kaiser's court. In 1898 the wild, high-spirited girl met the Englishman, Ernest Weekley, whom Aldous Huxley labeled "possibly the dullest professor in the western hemisphere," and much to the surprise of everyone who knew Frieda, she married the etymologist and went to live in the industrial setting of Nottingham where Weekley had been appointed a university lecturer. She had three children, a boy and two girls, a splendid home, and an automobile for her own use. But Frieda was bored and even her love affairs had little meaning for her. Lawrence was twenty-seven years old—Frieda, thirty-four and married twelve years—when he came to see his former professor about a teaching recommendation. Frieda may have been ready to give up her husband, but leaving her children was a torturous decision to make. There was no denying it: Lawrence woke what had been asleep in her for so long—a need for excitement and a renewed appetite for life.

But living with a different man didn't end her affairs. Frieda was amoral, sexually. Her unfaithfulness to Lawrence was frequent throughout their married life; even when they were first living together she made love to a woodcutter she didn't know, as David Garnett recalled, "just to show Lawrence she was free to do what she liked."[12] Sexual relations with Lawrence's friends, such as Middleton Murry, Cecil Gray, and Harold Hobson, and with Italian peasants, including Angelo Ravagli who would become her third husband, were carried on without much discretion. Frieda gave her sex generously. Yet she needed Lawrence and depended on him. He seemed more concerned about his own sexual life–particularly when she accused him of being impotent. Frieda's sexual behavior shocked her daughter, Barbara Weekley, at the time of Lawrence's death. Not only did Frieda share her bed with Murry and refuse to break her long affair with Ravagli, but according to Lawrence scholar Emile Delavenay, Frieda repeatedly locked her daughter in a bedroom with the Calabrian youth who had made the phoenix for Lawrence's grave at Vence to cure Barbara of "the fits of delirium and violent outbursts of hatred against her mother."[13] Two years before Lawrence's death, when Frieda returned home after seeing Angelo Ravagli again, Lawrence, who well knew what was going on, said to her: "Every heart has a right to its own secrets."

Frieda resented having to live in the shadow of Lawrence's mother, Lydia Lawrence. His attachment to his mother left him incapable of forming a normal relationship with other women. The mother always intervened. He expected other women to dress the way she did, to cook like her, and when he scrubbed floors he did them the way she had taught him. Her codes of propriety were his—the only explanation for the fact that the author of *Lady Chatterley's Lover* believed that sexual intercourse was indecent any time except in the middle of the night. His many domestic accomplishments—Stanley Hocking's old Cornish saying of being able to "wash, mend, bake and sew"— were learned in childhood to please his mother and to be useful to her.

Lawrence's mother, the young Lydia Beardsall, was impressed with Arthur Lawrence's black beard and his accomplishments on the dance floor. He made his work in the coal mines sound romantic, and his rustic ways and speech amused her. She had been a schoolmistress, had written verses, and had been jilted by a refined young man when the coal miner entered her life. They were happy together in the beginning of their marriage, but Arthur Lawrence broke his pledge and began stopping for beers with his friends at the pubs on his way home from work at night. She nagged and scolded him and the scenes turned ugly. There were children now, and the love she had felt for her husband was lavished on her offspring and against him. As Lawrence wrote Edward Garnett, November 14, 1912, when developing *Sons and Lovers*: "But as her sons grow up she selects them as lovers—first the eldest, then the second. These sons are *urged* into life by their reciprocal love of their mother—urged on and on. But when they come to manhood, they can't love, because their mother is the strongest power in their lives, and holds them."[14] Lawrence really wanted to fill the void in his mother's life by returning her love but such an undertaking was too much. It did indeed leave him incapable of accepting a woman's love and with a fear of women.

If Lawrence's mother hadn't died of cancer at the age of fifty-eight, in 1910, and had she lived another twenty years, surviving Lawrence who died in 1930, she probably would have overpowered him. But her death didn't free him. He tried to escape her when killing her symbolically in the writing of *Sons and Lovers*, by administering an overdose of medicine to mercifully end her suffering, but her ties were too tangled and deeply knotted. Frieda had to put up with his mother's death from the first, and after the symbolic killing to a lesser degree, but the loss was always there to come between them. Frieda didn't suppress her irritation. In a notebook where Lawrence kept his

poems, she once penned a message suggesting that he should go back
to his mother's apron strings. And another time she wrote a skit called
"Paul Morel, or His Mother's Darling." Lawrence read it, and in a
frosty voice declared: "This kind of thing isn't called a skit."[15]

Diana Trilling, in her introductioin to *Selected Letters of D. H.
Lawrence*, wrote that it was the combination of the war and his
marriage to Frieda that brought Lawrence close to a breakdown.
Lawrence should never have institutionalized their relationship. Live
with Frieda, yes. But once his sexual feelings for Frieda became a
"social regularity and conventional family emotion, it brought sex into
the established connection with love." Trilling suggested that Lawrence wanted Frieda to love him like a mother, but after the couple
were married, Frieda became "the very mother person from whom she
had supposed to detach him." Trilling felt that Lawrence needed "a
German woman like Frieda to stay entirely sane and make a successful
career of the lunacy" of their marriage.[16]

Frieda was hopelessly clumsy when faced with practical matters. The telephone was too much for her, and she was unable to do
the simplest of household chores with any competence. Even when
using words, though she was sensitive to them, she was never able to
express herself adequately. This led people to think of her as being
stupid and trivial. She was exceedingly tactless, and as Diana Trilling
assessed her: "a bit of a swamp, she had a swampy mind and spirit."[17]
Frieda was indolent, careless in her dress, and inclined to put on
weight. Cecily Lambert Minchin, who knew the Lawrences after
Cornwall, recalls: "I can see her now on that evening, sitting back on
a low arm chair, purring away like a lazy cat and shewing a great deal
of plump leg above the knee encased in calico bloomers probably
made by D. H. himself. She was not permitted to wear silk or
dainties."[18]

Frieda must have felt lonely from time to time throughout their
marriage. Many of Lawrence's friends were hostile to her, and the
demands Lawrence placed on her to fit his conception of their union
must have eroded some of Frieda's good humor. Lawrence had been
known to rudely dismiss the few friends she made on her own. She
rarely was able to see her children while they were growing up, and
they were told by their father, Ernest Weekley, that their mother
wasn't a worthy person and was best forgotten. Then there was the
death of her father, in addition to the many relations and childhood
acquaintances who were dying at the front in the German forces.

Lawrence's puritanism surfaced frequently. He may have sewed Frieda's calico bloomers himself, but he snarled at her for sitting with her legs apart. It was he who insisted that they get married for decency's sake. It is sometimes difficult to think of Lawrence as the apostle of our sexual revolution; the writer who wanted to make sex beautiful and not an act of shame; all this from a man who was an outright sexist. One never knew where Lawrence stood—he would recoil at the sight of exposed flesh and he would write about the sexual act with a boldness that shocked critics into charging him with pornography. He wasn't one who appreciated smutty stories. Lawrence disliked them intensely—the way his mother no doubt did—and he showed his displeasure whenever he heard them. But he didn't object to rank words being used to ornament or clarify a sentence. Frieda's enjoyment in taking whatever came her way with amoral gluttony often caused Lawrence's black moods to soar. She was the opposite of his mother in all her thoughts and actions.

Lawrence beat Frieda, he treated her shabbily before strangers and friends, but he was lost when she was away from him. She knew that much of his irritability came from illness, and she guarded his health valiantly while he continued to abuse her. Sometimes the gentle side of his nature astonished her—she once bumped her head against a shutter and he showed unusual concern and sympathy. But he would soon turn on her again and they would argue bitterly. "I am no Jesus that lies on his mother's lap," Lawrence wrote Baronin von Richthofen. "Oh, mother-in-law, you understand as my mother finally understood, that a man doesn't want, doesn't ask for love from his wife; but for strength, strength, strength. To fight, to fight, and to fight again."[19] This was written years after the Cornish episode, in 1923, when the Lawrences had learned some ground rules for their feuding. In Cornwall, a sickness overcame Lawrence. The most desperate battles of their marriage were fought at Tregerthen.

## IV

The possibility of having to serve in the military troubled Middleton Murry, but even more disturbing to him that spring were Lawrence's ideas of *Blutbruderschaft* and Katherine Mansfield's dislike for Tregerthen. Murry began to feel himself being pulled in two directions while the ground shifted under his feet. "With Katherine miserable I was half a man, wretchedly aware that she was only pretending to enter into our common concerns." The thought of Katherine Mansfield having to act a part sickened him. Murry had known what it was to be happy with her in their Villa Pauline at Bandol, and he felt himself caught between Katherine's dislike for what was going on around her and Lawrence's expectations of him as a friend. Murry didn't understand Lawrence's concept of an ideal community and friendship, though he could see that his friend needed him. "I knew how glad he had been that we had come, and I knew that I was glad to be with him again. I did not want to withdraw from him; but still less could I withdraw from Katherine."[1]

Murry believed that he could only feel sure of himself when he and Katherine were close and loving together. Take that away and he was left with only his deadly self-consciousness. Murry had to turn where his life was. Lawrence wouldn't accept the idea because he felt his marriage with Frieda left room and need for a relationship with a man and he insisted on having such a tie with Murry. When Murry felt whole he had no need of Lawrence. "I could love him tenderly and affectionately," Murry wrote, "as I believe I did, but I did not depend on him. If ever I did depend on him, it was because the relation between Katherine and me was not whole."[2]

Katherine Mansfield was frequently angered by Murry's inability to act on his own. She hated his self-pity and his ineptness as a lover—there were never any caresses and preliminaries in their love-making. More than once Katherine accused him of being "just like a little dog whining outside a door" and she called him "a little mole hung out on a string to dry."[3] Katherine knew Murry was too much under Lawrence's influence at Tregerthen, and she was determined to break the spell. Her resistance to the friendship between the two men caused Murry to back away from Lawrence and to grow closer to Katherine. Then the demands of a *Blutbruderschaft* became more urgent. Lawrence insisted there had to be a bond made between them and this could only be achieved by a sacrament performed on the dark Cornish moors. Such a blood rite frightened Murry, and Lawrence became more exasperated. Lawrence would turn against Frieda after being with Murry. "If I love you, and you know I love you, isn't that enough?" Murry asked his friend. And Lawrence proclaimed: "I hate your love, I *hate* it." Then one night the Murrys heard Lawrence shout to Frieda: "Jack is killing me."[4]

It was during this time that Lawrence was writing his novel *Women in Love*. When Murry read it four years later and wrote a hostile review of it, he was unaware that he was in the story. Only when Frieda told him that he and Katherine were included could he see that his and Lawrence's *blutbruder* conversations approximated those between Gerald Crich and Rupert Birkin. And he was Crich, Frieda pointed out. "Anyhow," Murry wrote, "that was a rough way of putting it; I was not Gerald Crich, but it probably is true that Lawrence found the germ of Gerald in me, as he found the germ of Gudrun in Katherine."[5]

Lawrence felt that Murry's relationship with Katherine was deadly. It didn't have the life-giving union that he had with Frieda. But Lawrence needed a new relationship with Murry to complete his marriage with Frieda. Rupert (Lawrence) tells Gerald (Murry): "You've got to take down the love-and-marriage ideal from its pedestal. We want something broader. I believe in the *additional* perfect relationship between man and man—additional to marriage."[6] Murry was convinced that Lawrence was undergoing a change at Tregerthen. Lawrence wasn't at all the unselfish man he had once known. "What he really wanted of me," Murry claimed, "he never put into words, and to this day I am doubtful whether he ever knew. But what he imagined he wanted is stated clearly in the novel."[7]

In *Women in Love* Rupert Birkin visited a very bored and edgy Gerald Crich. Gerald is delighted to see his friend. " 'By God, Rupert,' he said, 'I'd just come to the conclusion that nothing in the world mattered except somebody to take the edge off one's being alone: the right somebody.' " Perhaps a woman would be the solution, but failing that "an amusing man." The conversation turned to the possible cures for ennui. Birkin had found Japanese wrestling beneficial, but the best results could only be achieved by wrestling without clothing. The proposal fascinated Crich, and the two disrobed and began wrestling as their "bodies clinched into oneness." When Rupert realized that he had "fallen prostrate upon Gerald's body," he waited for his pounding heart "to become stiller and less painful." Birkin started to rise, and as he put out his hand to steady himself he touched Gerald's hand. The two gladiators clasped hands for a moment before dressing. " 'I think also that you are beautiful,' said Birkin to Gerald, 'and that is enjoyable too. One should enjoy what is given.' " Gerald asked if Birkin meant beautiful "physically" and his friend confessed how much he enjoyed Gerald's "northern kind of beauty, like light refracted from snow— and a beautiful, plastic form." Gerald now felt better and less edgy. "Is this the *Bruderschaft* you wanted?" asked Gerald. Birkin replied that it might be and wondered if it pledged anything. Gerald didn't know but both agreed that they felt "freer and more open."[8]

"Did you need Gerald?" Ursula (Frieda) asks on the closing page of *Women in Love,* and Birkin admits that he did. "Aren't I enough for you?" she asks. "You are enough for me, as far as woman is concerned," Birkin tells her. "But I wanted a man friend, as eternal as you and I are eternal." He could live all his life without a man friend, but to be really happy and to make life complete he needed an "eternal union" with a man. "You can't have two kinds of love." Ursula tells Birkin. "It seems as if I can't," Birkin replies. "Yet I wanted it."[9]

Frieda Lawrence insisted that her husband was never homosexual, but later in life she admitted that Lawrence "did not disbelieve in homosexuality." She was convinced that he and Murry never had a "love affair."[10] Professor Emile Delavenay, author of *D. H. Lawrence and Edward Carpenter,* in a letter of 30 June 1969, claimed that Frieda was very guarded in her remarks concerning all Cornish incidents at Higher Tregerthen and Tregerthen farm, that Frieda was busy creating the Lawrence legend as early as 1932, and that she was jealous of Lawrence and all his friends.[11]

"Was Lawrence homosexual?" Stanley Hocking repeated the question when asked. "Certainly not! Not to my knowledge. He may have been a bit effeminate. But I refuse to believe that Lawrence was homosexual. He already had a woman to dapple with." Other members of the Hocking family seemed uncomfortable when the question was raised. There had been talk of this within the family, and it was not something they were going to discuss at length with a stranger. Only one person within the circle of family and friends was willing to let drop a few words in response to the question—Arthur Eddy. His source of information didn't come from fashionable Bloomsbury gossip or interpretations of passages from Lawrence's writings; it came from William Henry Hocking. "I don't know if I ought to tell you this or not," said Arthur Eddy, "but William Henry told me one day that Lawrence was." ("Was homosexual?") "Yes, that's what William Henry told me. He said Lawrence used to come down to the farm and talk to him about it a lot."

Scottish composer and critic Cecil Gray described Lawrence's unpublished *Goats and Compasses,* a work Lawrence had completed shortly before coming to Tregerthen, as being Lawrence at his worst: "a bombastic, pseudo-mystical, psycho-philosophical treatise dealing largely with homosexuality—a subject, by the way, in which Lawrence displayed a suspiciously lively interest at that time." Gray claimed that there were two manuscript copies of the book. Lawrence destroyed the one copy he had, "while the other," which Philip Heseltine had in his possession, "was gradually consumed" by Heseltine "some years later, leaf by leaf, in the discharge of a lowly but none the less highly appropriate function. But the world need not be unduly perturbed at the loss; it was assuredly no masterpiece."[12]

Lawrence was always intimate with some woman—his mother established the need and it continued throughout his life. But he was never able to achieve any great intimacy with men. The male physique fascinated him, and he longed to form a bond with a male. He was fond of women, and terribly dependent on Frieda, though he never loved women beyond the spiritual love a man has for a sister. Repressed by a puritan environment while growing up, and wanting male friends and the camaraderie that his father enjoyed at the pits, Lawrence desired to form a tender male friendship which was beyond his emotional capacity. Idella Purnell Stone, who knew Lawrence in Mexico, in 1923, wrote Witter Bynner: "Psychologists say that we progress from mother to father worship, then to an incipient form of homosexuality or lesbianism, then to heterosexuality, at last to switch into the 'normal' channels. My own feeling about Lawrence is that he never got beyond the first step, and I think he knew it, that that was his deep trouble."[13]

Lawrence was a sickly child: quick to catch colds, frail, and unable to compete in strenuous games with boys his own age. He was often in the company of girls and forever in search of embracing male strength. He wanted a deep communion with a man as a source of renewal. In a letter of August 6, 1953, Frieda wrote Murry: "If he had lived longer and been older, you would have been real friends, he wanted so desperately for you to understand him. I think the homosexuality in him was a short phase out of misery—I fought him and won—and that he wanted a deeper thing from you."[14]

One wonders why a worldly Rupert Birkin should look to a shallow Gerald Crich for that relationship additional to marriage. What did Birkin see in him? And what did Lawrence see in Middleton Murry? Lawrence knew Murry's weaknesses: his inability to be decisive, his capacity for deception, and his high moral tone—Katherine Mansfield often called Murry "a monk without a monastery"; one who couldn't "fry a sausage without thinking about God."[15] Murry was easy to be with, but he was no German knight to rub cuts with and to pledge eternal love.

The semi-homosexual tie Lawrence tried to establish with Murry came at the time that Lawrence was demanding complete submission from Frieda. They had to be concurrent. As early as 1913, he wrote: "I believe a man projects his own image on another man, like on a mirror. But from a woman he wants himself re-born, re-constructed. So he can always get satisfaction from a man, but it is the hardest thing in life to get one's soul and body satisfied from a woman, so that one is free from oneself."[16] Lawrence was unsuccessful in both. Frieda wasn't about to conform to his expectations of submissiveness, and Murry was too unsettled by Katherine Mansfield's mood at Tregerthen to pledge himself on the Cornish moors. It was Lawrence's inability to establish the kind of relationships he wanted that kindled his violent rages and brought him close to the breaking point.

Lawrence wanted a man friend all his life and never was the need greater than during the war years in Cornwall. The intense feelings Lawrence had for Murry were showered on William Henry Hocking when it became obvious that Katherine Mansfield had won in the struggle over Murry. Aside from the friendship with William Henry, visiting the Hockings was in many ways for Lawrence a return to the Haggs farm and the Chambers family—a farm only two miles from Lawrence's boyhood home in Eastwood. "Bert" Lawrence loved the Chambers family, and he was often with them (as described in his novels, *The White Peacock* and *Sons and Lovers*) playing charades, carrying on high-spirited conversations, and helping in the fields with the harvest. "Work goes like fun when Bert's there," said Mr. Chambers. And Mrs. Chambers declared: "I should like to be next to Bert in heaven."[17] Lawrence loved to be with the two older Chambers boys, Alan and Hubert, and later with Jessie, the sensitive young girl who soon wanted more education after meeting the young Bert. In a letter to J. D. Chambers, youngest son of the Chambers family, written in

November 1928, Lawrence looked back on those early days. "Whatever I forget, I shall never forget the Haggs—I loved it so. I loved to come to you all, it really was a new life began in me there." And Lawrence concluded: "If there is anything I can ever do for you, do tell me—Because whatever else I am, I am somewhere still the same Bert who rushed with such joy to the Haggs."[18]

Lawrence's favorite was Alan Chambers, and he was with his farm friend often, working in the hay and helping with the chores. In Lawrence's first novel, *The White Peacock*, 1911, Cyril, the Lawrence figure, declares that his friendship with George Saxton (Alan Chambers) was "more perfect than any love I have known since, either for man or woman."[19] And in a discarded prologue to *Women in Love*, Lawrence is more explicit. His feelings are clearly expressed in Rupert Birkin's response: "All the time, he recognized that, although he was always drawn to women, feeling more at home with a woman than with a man, yet it was for men that he felt the hot, flushing roused attraction which a man is supposed to feel for the other sex."[20]

Lawrence loved Alan Chambers, and the young farmer was fond of his friend and impressed with Lawrence's knowledge of the world. But illness, and Lydia Lawrence's jealousy when she became aware of Jessie Chambers' interest in her son, kept Lawrence more and more away from the Haggs and his male companion. In *Sons and Lovers*, Paul Morel tells Miriam that if only she had been a man their relationship would have been ideal. The comment didn't go unnoticed by Miriam. She knew of his longing for a profound friendship with her elder brother. And a parallel situation developed at Tregerthen. Frieda, the mother figure, was jealous of her Bert's intense interest, not in a Jessie this time, but in the new Alan Chambers—William Henry.

The handsome Tregerthen farmer wasn't characterized in *Women in Love*, but he is clearly brought to mind in the unused prologue. "There would come into a restaurant a strange Cornish type of man, with dark eyes like holes in his head, or like the eyes of a rat, and with dark, fine, rather stiff hair, and full, heavy, softly-strong limbs. Then again Birkin would feel the desire spring up in him, the desire to know this man, to have him, as it were to eat him, to take the very substance of him. And watching the strange, rather furtive, rabbit-like way in which the strong, softly-built man ate, Birkin would feel the rousedness burning in his own breast, as if this were what he wanted, as if the satisfaction of his desire lay in the body of the young, strong man opposite."[21] Fiction isn't reality, even if this discarded section does read more like a prologue for men in love. But Lawrence did pack the pages of his fiction with clear, and often cruel, descriptions of people he met casually or knew well. The "Cornish type of man" Lawrence described is an accurate snapshot of William Henry, a true likeness which even catches a gesture or two of the man as he sits eating at the table.

"Was there really a thing between them?" Mabel Dodge Luhan claimed to have asked Frieda in 1922. And Frieda replied: "I think so. I was dreadfully unhappy."[22] One can imagine the scene of seduction—perhaps somewhere in the darkness on the shaggy moors where the Druidical boulders suggest a blood ceremony. But it would be only speculation; no evidence had been unearthed to confirm such a culmination. And we can't expect a "stout-hearted" farmer to react in the same way as a well-educated and indecisive John Middleton Murry. Land and animals were Hocking's principal concerns. Out of nowhere, Lawrence appeared, and he understood Hocking's fear of death. Then the two talked of dying and the powers of death and William Henry was wide awake to the wonders of the unknown. A curious selfishness kept their relationship alive as Lawrence spoke of blood-consciousness—Lawrence probing, Hocking misunderstanding and intentionally misunderstanding. It would have been impossible for William Henry to accept all that Lawrence suggested. Lawrence's *blutbruder* probes went far beyond William Henry's comprehension, but Hocking did little to discourage his friend. In fact, he coaxed Lawrence on, and both men felt renewed as Lawrence reiterated his ideas on blood sacrifice.

Catherine Carswell, in her *The Savage Pilgrimage*, wrote: "I have heard Lawrence say that sexual perversion was for him 'the sin against the Holy Ghost,' the hopeless sin." Lawrence assured Carswell that his relationship with Hocking was "no sin against the Holy Ghost."[23] He often expressed his aversion to homosexuality—sometimes so vehemently that one wonders why all the commotion, as when he wrote Koteliansky in 1915: "We have had another influx of visitors: David Garnett and Francis Birrell turned up the other day—Saturday. I like David, but Birrell I have come to detest. These horrible little frowsty people, men lovers of men, they give me such a sense of corruption, almost putrescence, that I dream of beetles."[24]

For Katherine Mansfield, another problem at Higher Tregerthen was Lawrence's obsession with sexual symbolism and man's animal nature. Mansfield was unable to see phallic comparisons in trees, brooks, and pen fillers. Mansfield suggested to Lawrence that he should call his cottage "The Phallus" and Frieda was quick to agree. It is interesting to note how the name "John Thomas" appears and reappears in Lawrence's fiction: William Henry Hocking was characterized as "John Thomas Buryan of Trendrinnan farm" in "The Nightmare" chapter of *Kangaroo;* it was used for the tram conductor in the short story "Tickets Please"; and the second draft of *Lady Chatterley's Lover*, later to be published, was called *John Thomas and Lady Jane.* "John Thomas," Lawrence wrote Mabel Luhan, "is one of the names for the penis, as you probably know."[25]

The tension was unbearable for Middleton Murry as he fought to escape Lawrence. Murry was just beginning to be heard as a critic at the time, and the rather barren landscape of Tregerthen was not the ideal place for one who wanted to be in touch with the London literary crowd. But there were "peaceful and happy interludes," Murry recalled, as when the Spanish ship, the *Manu,* "ran aground on the rocks below," when they all went to "cottage sales" and placed bids for bargains, or drove together over the moors to Penzance and journeyed to Marazion where they found shells. "But they were interludes of convalescence, mere intervals in a struggle which was wearing us down to the naked nerves."[26]

Stanley Hocking recalled the *Manu* incident. "A few days after the Spanish steamer *Manu* was wrecked in our cove, some of the Spanish sailors came back to see their old ship. I remember my mother giving them tea, and Lawrence and Murry came down to have a chat with them. Lawrence tried to talk to them in Spanish, the few words he knew, but he couldn't get much sense out of them. Then he tried them in French, and they all talked a bit. After the sailors had left, Lawrence said to us: 'That's funny. Those fellows can talk a better French than Spanish!' "

The excursion to Marazion convinced Katherine Mansfield that she and Murry must move to the kindly south side of the Cornish coast. They told Lawrence their plans, using the excuse that Katherine "felt herself in a foreign country" on the northern shore. Lawrence heard them with "unmoved indifference," but they weren't deceived. Then late one night Murry heard Lawrence crying to Frieda that Murry was "an obscene bug that was sucking his life away," and Murry's blood turned cold. "Again, I will not pretend," Murry wrote, "that I cannot now find a meaning in his feeling; it was not simply, as

I then felt, the raging of some awful mania. But now as then, it horrifies me that Lawrence should have been in a condition in which his feeling sought such words."[27]

Murry went looking for a cottage, and found one at Mylor, along a creek of the Truro River, for 18 pounds a year. They lost no time in moving. Katherine Mansfield went on ahead by train and Murry hired a cart to move their belongings. "It would have been unlike Lawrence, even at such a moment, not to have lent a hand; and he did. But our hearts were sore."[28] Lawrence refused to say good-bye. Frieda took it all lightly; she said she would visit them. When Murry went up the lane on his bicycle he felt that he had left Lawrence forever.

V

Lawrence's letters to friends during the spring of 1916 made no mention of the rows with Frieda and the struggle with Murry, but they did reveal a tormented man who felt despair when his thoughts turned to the war. Lawrence maintained that the possibility of being conscripted under the new Military Service Act bored him, though his letters clearly showed this to be otherwise. "We have had several copies of the *Berliner Tageblatt*," he wrote Lady Ottoline Morrell. Lawrence and Frieda, hungry for news from the continent, read the German newspapers with much interest. "Germany seems queer: she seems to have got over her great anti-Christian, anti-democratic outburst, her great rage of sheer reaction in which she burst upon us." Lawrence felt the battle lines were wrong. The fight should be at home. "England fighting England. This is what it ought to be, in the fight to a finish. But this is what it won't be, if Col. Churchill and Co. have their own way. We shall all be whipped up like dogs to fasten on the body of Germany."[1]

The local postman, who doubled as a Wesleyan preacher in St. Ives, was also interested in the German newspapers. He didn't like Frieda because of her German accent and he mistrusted men who wore beards. Parcels of newspapers bearing Swiss stamps probably would have been suspicious items for any postman delivering mail in a small town in wartime England. In "The Nightmare" chapter of *Kangaroo*, Lawrence wrote that the Cornish postman "had a religious zest added to his natural Cornish zest" of enjoying "other people's disasters," and the "thought of hell for other men was sweet in him."[2]

"I'm not so sure his zest was Cornish," said Stanley Hocking, "but it's a very good way of putting it. I think there was a certain hostility between the two, and Lawrence felt a bit uncomfortable when the man came to the door. But the postman and Lawrence shied away from each other. I know that postman would give a grin when he came with those wretched envelopes calling a person to war." P. O. Eddy also recalled this deliverer of tidings. "There used to be a little postbox where people could pick up their letters, down the lane, near Lawrence's cottage. I know I went out once to give a letter to this postman. I thought I would just hand him the letter. But he wouldn't take it until I had put it in the postbox. A very peculiar fellow, he was. He was a preacher, and a good one."

"Unfortunately the Murrys do not like the country—it is too rocky and bleak for them," Lawrence wrote Lady Ottoline. "They should have a soft valley, with leaves and the ring-dove cooing. And this is a hillside of rocks and magpies and foxes." Then Lawrence observed that the walls of the Murrys' tower cottage were wet from the heavy rains, but the problem could be corrected. "I am very sorry they don't like it, because I like this country and my little cottage so much. I think I shall always keep this cottage."[3]

Lawrence's grave doubts concerning the war didn't halt his progress with *Women in Love*. He began writing the book late in April and by May 24 he was able to report to Lady Ottoline that the new novel was coming rapidly and that it was good. "When one is shaken to the very depths, one finds reality in the unreal world." His present world was his "inner soul," and the "outer world is there to be endured" but it wasn't real.[4]

The north shore of Cornwall was too wild for the Murrys, Lawrence wrote Catherine Carswell on June 19. And he and Murry weren't true associates. "I was angry when you ran over a list of my 'friends'—whom you did *not* think much of. But it is true, they are not much, any of them." Then Lawrence announced that he was through with having friends who were intimate. It was deceiving himself to have such friendships. And in the same letter, Lawrence wrote: "I have no particular news: except that I have to go and join the colours in Penzance on the 28th. I shall go, and take my chances of being accepted. If I must be a soldier, then I must—ta-rattata-ta! It's no use trying to dodge one's fate."[5] The preacher-postman had smilingly handed Lawrence the dreaded "On His Majesty's Service" envelope at last! "Envelopes which summon a man for torture," Lawrence told the Hockings.

He reported to the military authorities in Penzance, and Frieda rode over the moors with him in Tom Berryman's wagon. Much to Lawrence's surprise, he was ordered to proceed to Bodmin, in central Cornwall, for his physical examination. He said good-bye to Frieda, and Berryman drove her back to the lonely cottage at Tregerthen. On the sixty-mile train trip to Bodmin the other recruits sang all the patriotic and sentimental songs of a nation at war. They were lined up on the station platform and marched through the streets of Bodmin to the barracks. "Like convicts," Lawrence told the Hockings. He felt the camaraderie of the men was a degradation. It was losing one's individuality and becoming part of the mob spirit. He liked the men who went with him, though he believed they had made a mistake by choosing to serve. Answering the colors when called was one thing but enlisting was another. They were all brave men, yet not one was capable of rejecting suffering. They were too willing to accept their miseries without demanding happiness. Lawrence thought this a loss of integrity. They must stand by their fellow men and be slaughtered. It was all too depressing for him. "This is what Christ's weeping over Jerusalem has brought us to, a whole Jerusalem offering itself to the Cross," he wrote Catherine Carswell. "This is the most terrible madness."[6] At all cost, he wouldn't serve. Lawrence was keenly aware of how different he looked—a man with a beard. He sensed his isolation, and his beard became a symbol. If it had to be taken off, he would be defeated. It represented his independent manhood.

They all slept that night in Bodmin. The barracks seemed like a prison to Lawrence and he was reminded of Oscar Wilde in Reading Gaol. The food was bad but the sergeant was likable. Lawrence was ashamed of the patches on his underwear—he was so poor. He slept badly that night, kept awake by one man's cough and the groans of some men in their sleep. At dawn came the rush to the icy baths, the revolting breakfast, and the order to tidy the barracks. Lawrence was called "Dad" because of his beard. Then the physical examination. He stood while the doctors probed and asked their questions. Lawrence wasn't strong, and the doctors declared him unfit for service. But he was told to find some form of volunteer service. He kept silent, knowing this he wouldn't do. The other men looked at him resentfully because they thought he had been favored—he wasn't a working man. Lawrence had won his reprieve; for a time he would be safe; he was free. He hurried back to Tregerthen to relate his experiences to an anxious Frieda. They were both jubilant.

"Lawrence came down and told us how he had been treated when he got back from Bodmin," said Stanley Hocking. " 'A ghastly experience,' Lawrence said. 'Most degrading to have to hop to and fro, stark naked in a room before a half-dozen doctors.' He didn't like that. He wasn't passed very high that time in Bodmin. He said to me after he came back: 'They will never make a soldier out of me.' He said he hated the whole thing. 'I don't want to go and fight and kill anybody. And if the Germans come here and want my little cottage, they can have it. I wouldn't kill them.' Compulsion is never appealing to us Cornish," Hocking explained. "I don't think anybody wanted to go. The war was so far away, and as soon as anyone left a farm the whole way of life was disrupted. On a farm there are certain jobs to be done every day. If you have dairy cattle, sheep, horses and pigs, they must be fed and looked after every day. And when one person from the family is missing, who is going to do his work? It's either trying to replace that person with someone else, which would be rather impossible, or asking all the others to do a lot extra."

With the Bodmin ordeal behind him and the Murrys gone, Lawrence became more interested in his surroundings. The war still depressed him, but he felt this was a time for rejoicing. He planned little excursions to Penzance and Land's End, and he was frequently at the farm helping the Hockings in the fields. Lawrence and Frieda liked Katie Berryman who ran the grocery shop in Zennor village. They were fond of her saffron cakes and buns, and they enjoyed the local gossip which circulated freely in this combination grocery and post office. Katie Berryman's husband, Tom, was in charge of the mail, and the Lawrences often hired him and his wagon for their local adventures.

His novel had come rushing out. By late June he had nearly completed it. Lawrence had decided to type the book himself—on a typewriter Amy Lowell had given him. He sent a message to J. B. Pinker, his London literary agent, saying he would type the novel within six weeks, and would Pinker send him money? Lawrence felt he could live on one hundred and fifty pounds a year at Tregerthen. But his agent was slow in responding, and on July 12, he wrote Pinker again telling him he had only six pounds. His request for funds crossed with Pinker's reply, for Lawrence wrote his agent the following day thanking him for a fifty pound check.

Lawrence had decided to keep the tower part of the cottage left empty by the Murrys. "It is *so* near," he wrote Catherine Carswell, "that if strangers came, it would be intolerable. So I am buying a very little furniture—it is so cheap and *so* nice here, second-hand—to furnish a sitting-room and a bedroom, for the visitors." Invitations went out to Catherine Carswell, Dollie Radford, and Barbara Low. They must come and see Tregerthen for themselves. "I expect Dollie and Maitland Radford for a few days—a week or so—somewhere about the 20th," he wrote Barbara Low on July 8. "When does your holiday begin? Your room will be ready for you."[7] Then Lawrence began struggling with Captain Short for a mason to roof the tower with new slate and to install gutters. The tower cottage had to be made watertight. Lawrence was now convinced that the dampness of the walls was the reason for the Murrys' departure.

He wrote Katherine Mansfield on July 16—she had just returned to Mylor after a visit to London. "We will come to Mylor at your disposal, on a sunny day." The weather had been bad and Lawrence had been feeling shaky. "Dollie Radford comes here on the 31st; after her, Beresford, and I expect, Barbara Low. So August is done for. Let me know what day will suit you, between now and the 31st." He wondered why Murry hadn't answered his letter or penned a message with the money he sent Lawrence for settling a cottage expense. Lawrence shared some of the local gossip and sent an enthusiastic report on the height of the corn and the splendor of the Tregerthen moors. "Really, one should find a place one can live in, and stay there. Geographical change doesn't help one much. And people go from bad to worse. I think I shall be staring out from Higher Tregerthen when I am a nice old man of seventy."[8]

Lawrence and Frieda crossed on the ferry from Penrhyn to Mylor. Middleton Murry remembered Lawrence arriving, wearing his "white linen sun-hat" and carrying a rucksack and showing his "apostolic contempt" for the soft, dove-cooing lands south of Tregerthen. They all went on a picnic in a dinghy, but after lunch the skies turned gray and windy, and they started back with Lawrence at the oars. "Like a slim St. Peter, Lawrence put his back into it; but he was no waterman," Murry observed in *Between Two Worlds*. "Worse still, he was no swimmer, neither was Frieda." They all became frightened because the small boat was overloaded, and with Lawrence pulling unevenly at the oars they had difficulty heading the dinghy into the wind. Murry was alarmed, but after a long struggle they got back to the shelter of Mylor Creek and could laugh at their escape. What could have been a disaster for the foursome failed to draw the two men closer. "One of my moods of self-sufficiency was upon me," Murry recalled. "But I certainly do not remember that my hostility to him was greater than his to me." His acceptance of the difference of their ways annoyed Lawrence; yet Murry didn't see why they couldn't be friends. "My persistence in this attitude made him furious; and he irritated me by showing contempt for what I offered."[9] The visit was far from being a success, and it was obvious to them both that they were further apart than ever. Katherine Mansfield remembered the leave-taking. "We walked him as far as the ferry and away he sailed in a little open boat pulled by an old, old man." Mansfield wrote Lady Ottoline Morrell that Lawrence "looked rather as though the people of Falmouth had cried to him as the Macedonians did to Paul and he was on his way over to help them."[10]

Even with Murry no longer at Higher Tregerthen to whip him into a frenzy, Lawrence still turned on Frieda viciously, particularly when she spoke longingly of her three children. He would feel threatened at the mere mention of their names, and he would be filled with jealousy. The fact that Frieda wasn't allowed to see her children officially and could only catch glimpses of them on London streets made it nearly unbearable for her. But Lawrence refused to concede this point. She had been without them for four years—she had lived with him—and he was more important to her than offspring. But when they argued about Monty, Elsa and Barbara, she resisted him with all her strength. When Frieda felt like weeping she wept, and whenever she thought about her children she began to cry. This sent Lawrence into a fury. He sometimes tongue-lashed her so brutally over the children that onlookers were aghast. He also tried another form of attack. He would tell her that it served her right to lose her children and that she should suffer for having abandoned them.

Lawrence had begun typing *Women in Love,* but he soon found the task made him nervous. He wrote J. B. Pinker, on July 21, wondering if the manuscript could be typed in Pinker's office. "I've not been well these last few weeks—so much wetness everywhere, I suppose. If I can, I will go to Italy another year." Lawrence was writing his fourth and final draft of the book and it was nearly finished. "When

I have done the novel I shall *only* write stories to *sell.* I hate getting further into debt. Heaven knows what you will think of the novel. I shall soon want some more money: not at once, but very soon."[11]

"He wouldn't say anything about his health," replied Stanley Hocking when asked about Lawrence's frequent bouts with illness at Tregerthen. "The only thing he would admit to was that he had a bad cold occasionally. Lawrence's health may have deteriorated quite a bit after he left us in October 1917, but I can say that he certainly showed no signs of consumption. He would have a touch of bronchitis, or a nasty cold or two that left him indisposed for a few days, but there was never much wrong with him." And Ivor Short recalled: "He was strong enough to go down and give the Hockings a hand on the farm. He wasn't crippled by any means. And he didn't look a weakling." But P. O. Eddy admitted: "He didn't have the strength that we Zennor lads have. He was a frail man."

"I am always seedy nowadays—my old winter sickness and inflammation—" Lawrence had written the Murrys from Padstow, Cornwall, shortly before coming to Tregerthen.[12] His right side had felt numb, and it was difficult for him to hold a pen. Dollie Radford's son, Dr. Maitland Radford, had come down from London to examine him. Dr. Radford found no evidence of tuberculosis, only congestion and inflammation, but this was one of the many times in Lawrence's life when his weak lungs caused him and Frieda to be concerned. Dr. Andrew Morland, the lung specialist who examined him shortly before his death, felt it was difficult to determine just when the tuberculosis began. Dr. Morland guessed a few months before the first hemorrhage in the mid-nineteen-twenties. Lawrence never allowed his illness to get the upper hand and destroy his optimism. It was only a cold or a slight bronchial disorder. Nothing alarming, he would declare—even when his lungs were nearly gone and he could barely drag himself up steps or go on short walks. But his weak chest was always a source of annoyance to him, and probably his struggle with poor health would explain many of his unexpected attacks on Frieda and his uneven temper.

Murry's first book of criticism, *Fydor Dostoievsky,* was published in July 1916, and he sent Lawrence a copy. Lawrence wrote and thanked him. "I have only just looked in it here and there—and read the epilogue." Lawrence wondered if anybody was ready to face the old life. "An epoch of the human mind may have come to the end in Dostoevsky: but humanity is capable of going on a very long way further yet, in a state of mindlessness—curse it." He felt that Murry had "got the cart before the horse." Not the being that follows the mind, but the mind that follows the being. He hastened to assure Murry that Dostoevsky, "like the rest, can nicely stick his head between the feet of Christ, and waggle his behind in the air. And though the behind-wagglings are a revelation, I don't think much even of the feet of Christ as a bluff for the cowards to hide their eyes against."[13] Recalling this letter, Murry felt Lawrence wanted to insult him, that he had criticized his book without reading it and had shown contempt for one of Murry's heroes. "I didn't mind so much as I would have done a year before. There was now something in me that could stand up to him."[14] The book was Murry's first literary success and its reception went far to free him from Lawrence. In his Dostoevsky letter to Murry, Lawrence concluded: "You want to be left alone—so do I—by everybody, by the whole world, which is despicable and contemptible to me and sickening."

First Dollie Radford, then Barbara Low came to Higher Tregerthen in August for short visits. They were put up in the refurnished tower part of the Murrys' cottage, and Lawrence took them on tours of the surrounding countryside. Stanley Hocking didn't recall Dollie Radford—"I do remember Catherine Carswell and Barbara Low. But we weren't particularly interested in whom the Lawrences had for visitors. They would come down at the farm with Lawrence when he came for his drop of milk. Typical city people; people who lived in a different world. I never got into conversation with Barbara Low or Catherine Carswell. They were just introduced as friends of the Lawrences."

With Murry gone, Lawrence began spending more time at the farm with William Henry and the Hockings. In the beginning, when Murry was still at Higher Tregerthen, Lawrence would "come and go" with the handsome Cornish farmer. It wasn't until the spring of 1917 that the friendship became intense, though Lawrence was full of William Henry when writing to his London friends as early as September 1916. Ill health and Frieda's reluctance to mix with the nearby farm family may have delayed Lawrence's drifting back to his newfound Haggs. He loved working in the fields with his friend and the two Hocking girls, Mabel and Mary. Lawrence's visits became more frequent as time passed, and he and William Henry "would linger putting up the sheaves, linger talking, till dark, talking of the half-mystical things with which they both were filled."[15]

## VI

The postmortem memoirs written by Lawrence's literary friends in the nineteen thirties, memoirs blaming the Cornish and the Hocking family for Lawrence's expulsion from the area, made lively reading. These reports were accepted and the obvious distortions weren't questioned. Scholars did visit Higher Tregerthen to see the little cottage where Lawrence had lived, but few made the effort of questioning the local people who had known Lawrence. One visitor was unimpressed when a St. Ives resident offered to introduce him to William Henry Hocking. The man declined, yet he had come to Cornwall to gather new material. Lawrence's cottage depressed still another stranger, and he hurriedly left Tregerthen, relieved that the pilgrimage was over.

The Hocking family became increasingly reluctant to talk to strangers about Lawrence with the passing years. If William Henry had been approached differently before a lingering disease overcame him—probably Alzheimer's—perhaps some of the Cornish mystery would have been brought into the open. Journalists should have asked William Henry how much hay he was cutting to the acre and how much manure was being plowed under for crops at Tregerthen before bringing up the subject of Lawrence. The few outsiders who did meet with the Hockings were only interested in D. H. Lawrence, the literary man, not the friend who came into the kitchen and sat talking by the old Cornish slab.

The major interview with the Hockings was aired on November 14 and 22, 1953, with questions posed by Brenda Hamilton and Tony Soper of the Bristol branch of the BBC."[1] The Hockings felt terribly uncomfortable throughout these two telediphone conversations—they came across like barnyard folk, not overly alert but splashing plenty of local color. Stanley Hocking's ability to use words colorfully and his uncanny way of recalling incidents from the past were missing. William Henry was disoriented because of his illness, and the sisters, Mabel and Mary, were vague when answering questions.

Why were the Hockings and Lawrence so close? It had to be more than a return to the Haggs. And what kind of a person was William Henry? Was he truly an unreliable nonentity who failed Lawrence in the end? Biographer Harry T. Moore suggested it, as did several of Lawrence's London friends.

"There was no one around that Lawrence could mix with," claimed Arthur Eddy. "I suppose Lawrence and William Henry had things in common. William Henry was very well liked, and he spent a lot of time reading. He had a lot of fun in him."

But Ivor Short declared: "What kind of a person is a Cornish farmer? And there you are. William Henry was an ordinary Cornish farmer. He couldn't sit down and talk like we're talking. He could talk about farming. He could tell you about cattle and sheep, but when it came to talking about other things it was a different matter. But Lawrence and William Henry were great pals. I don't know how it came about."

"Oh, William Henry could talk. He could do that," P. O. Eddy insisted. "That was the reason why William Henry and Lawrence were such friends. Lawrence wouldn't have become friends with other farmers the way he did with William Henry." And H. H. Hocking explained: "I think my father felt that Lawrence was a man in search of something and hadn't found it yet."

The two men would sit together long after the others at the farm had gone to bed: Lawrence talking with his friend "who loved a half-philosophical, mystical talking about the sun, and the moon, the mysterious change in man with the change of season, and the mysterious effects of sex on a man."[2] Lawrence knew his friend was not educated, but he believed that William Henry understood, even understood more than he did.

"Lawrence was no clock-watcher," claimed Stanley Hocking, "and neither was William Henry. If Lawrence had been up in the fields helping with the harvest, he would come in for supper that night at the farm and stay talking with William Henry until half past ten or midnight. I know they liked to exchange views about everything. Lawrence thought William Henry was more intelligent than the ordinary Cornish farmer."

"Lawrence was an influence in William Henry's life—to a certain extent," said Arthur Eddy. "When William Henry found someone who could talk he would get all he could out of that person. I suppose this was what he did when he talked with Lawrence. William Henry was curious about things. If he had been living in this day and age, he would have had an education. But in those days there was no opportunity."

In a letter to Barbara Low, on 20 August 1916, after Low's visit to Tregerthen, Frieda expressed concern for Lawrence's friend. "We are worried about William Henry, he is really interesting, we want him to have a 'lady' what would take an interest in him—" Lawrence broke into the letter at this point with the plan of sharing the Tregerthen farmer with London friends. "I like Frieda's suddenly conspiring to marry off poor William Henry. He is desirous of the intellectual life, and yet he isn't in the least fit for anything but his farming. Perhaps during the winter I shall get him to go to London for a few days: then Dollie, and you, and Mrs. Eder must look after him a bit." Lawrence felt there wasn't enough "mental continuity" to fling the Cornishman into the complexities of an intellectual life. It would require more than one generation for a man of such sensuous nature. "And he suffers *badly*, and his people hate him—because he *will* take the intellectual attitude, and they want only the vague sensuous non-critical." Lawrence believed his friend should break away from the family and live in one of the cottages next to him at Higher Tregerthen. "He looks to me as if I could suddenly give him wings—and it is a trouble and a nuisance."[3]

One wonders how enthusiastic Lawrence's friends were when they learned that they must assume the responsibility of making William Henry's debut on the London scene a success. Lawrence was quick to tell them that he was involved because he felt sorry for the man. He wasn't ready to admit how friendly the two had become, but the friendship was intense enough to convince Frieda that William Henry needed a woman. "It was a bitter time," for Frieda, Lawrence wrote in "The Nightmare" chapter of *Kangaroo*. To her, "with her pure Teutonic consciousness," William Henry's "greeting would sound like a jeer, as he called to her." And Lawrence would come back to her "like an enemy, with that look on his face, and that pregnant malevolency of Cornwall investing him."[4]

"Frieda was often alone in the cottage," admitted Stanley Hocking. "She rather liked Lawrence going out in the daytime. It gave her more freedom when he wasn't around all the time. On fine days, Lawrence would be out helping us or tending his garden. This arrangement was quite suitable for Frieda. But she didn't like being left alone in the evening. If Lawrence quarreled with Frieda, it was probably before he came down to see us. He used to come down on numerous occasions, in addition to giving me French lessons at the farmhouse table. I remember one particular night he came down when we didn't really expect him. But mother was rather wide awake when he came down on a rough night. I remember my mother saying to me before I had my lesson: 'They had a row this evening. That's why he's down here.' It was a wild and stormy night. In the midst of my French lesson, an occasional peal of thunder. Frieda was up in the cottage alone, and she got scared. She ran down to the farm and knocked loudly at the door, shouting: 'Lorenzo, Lorenzo, where are you? Why do you leave me alone on such a night as this?' So Lawrence packed up his books and went home with her."

In another letter to Barbara Low, on September 1, Lawrence wondered why Low was "so cross over Wm Hy." Perhaps she had little patience for entertaining Lawrence's friend in London—she hadn't met the farmer on her visit to Tregerthen. "I wish one didn't always find a petty tragedy on one's doorstep—It wasn't that I wouldn't let you see him, here—it was that one *does* avoid him," Lawrence explained, "he *is* rather a burden."[5] Lawrence claimed that William Henry hadn't been inside the house once, and for some unknown reason, he was unable to ask him. But it would be good if she would show William Henry around; it might help him to survive the winter spiritually; and he needed to have associations with other people. But the visit wouldn't be until harvest was over in October, just before turnip-pulling time.

"William Henry wants very much to come to London," Lawrence wrote Dollie Radford on September 5, "when harvest is over—next month, perhaps. Would you see him, and help to look after him, you and Margaret and Hester—if she is in town?" William Henry was filled with seeing the searchlights—he thought he could break away and make the visit. Lawrence doubted if his friend would move at all, knowing how slow William Henry was in getting to the harvest. "There is a great deal of friction down at the farm: the poor 'rascal and villain!' (Stanley and William Henry)—You knew that son-in-law, Hollow, was dead—three weeks ago. He went very rapidly. Mrs. Hocking is just beginning to cheer up a little."[6] The son-in-law died of tuberculosis, and six years later his wife, Katie, next to the oldest of the four Hocking girls, died from the same disease. In addition to sickness and grief, Mrs. Hocking was also being plagued by bickering in the household because of William Henry's unusual ways of conducting farm business.

"I suppose there was some friction down at the farm," said Arthur Eddy. "I know William Henry's sisters, Mabel and Mary, and his brother, Stanley, didn't appreciate him as much as they should have." The two sisters found much to criticize in their eldest brother's irregular hours. His habit of beginning the farm day late in the morning was looked upon as laziness. "William Henry wouldn't start work the time the others did," P. O. Eddy recalled, "and then he would be working until long after dark. He never went to bed before midnight. He was an unusual Cornish farmer. Cornish farmers are very alert in the morning," explained Mr. Eddy. "They haven't a name for stopping in bed."

"Time didn't mean anything to Father," said H. H. Hocking. "I remember we were working in the yard one day and it was dinner time and I was starving. I said: 'Come on, Father, let's go in to dinner.' He stopped and looked at me and said: 'Let me tell you, Son, never put off until tomorrow what you can do today, and never put off till after dinner what you can do before.' This was the way he was. But Father was always late with one exception. To my knowledge, he was never late to a funeral. Everything else would have to wait when he paid his last respects to a person."

Lawrence soon included William Henry in his Rananim plans. Even after Lawrence had left Cornwall and was staying in London, he wrote Catherine Carswell, in November 1917, of settling near "the east slope of the Andes, back of Paraguay or Columbia"—William Henry's name conspicuously appearing on a list with several of Lawrence's old friends.[7] Hocking's dissatisfaction with his life and style of living at the time was such that he allowed himself a share in Lawrence's dream of founding a colony. Not that William Henry would ever leave Cornwall. His greatest adventure into the world was already behind him: a trip to Salisbury Plain with the Home Guards, in 1912. But Hocking enjoyed the thought of one day associating with all the educated people his strange friend knew, and Lawrence was only too glad to include William Henry because it brought them closer together.

"Lawrence had an imaginary place which he was calling Rananim," Stanley Hocking recalled. "He thought it would be a good idea if they went into another country and founded a little colony where they could all live happily ever after. Lawrence talked a lot about this. But I don't think anyone can live on imagination. You need something to eat and drink. But apparently this wasn't considered. And I think William Henry was thinking that the whole thing was nonsense, and he wasn't having anything to do with it. After all, you can't leave a farm. You can't pack up and leave your animals and relatives and go somewhere to an imaginary place."

Lawrence kept his friend on the Rananim list, but he was soon disappointed in Hocking—William Henry didn't answer letters. As early as November 6, 1917, Lawrence wrote Cecil Gray: "I believe it is true, Mrs. Hocking misses us most. As for William Henry, sarà come sarà: he does as he likes, either Popayan-wards or otherwards."[8] The disenchantment was complete by July 3, 1918. He complained to Gray again: "What Zennor ructions—W H married, Katie going away: what will be left of Zennor? W. H. is rather a fool, and bores me. I feel distressed for the old ewe—his mother." Lawrence felt William Henry should leave the farm, and he would tell the Hockings that when they next wrote to him. It was all too much for him, and "there should be a general extirpation of the race."[9]

Lawrence was never able to see William Henry clearly as a person. He used the Cornishman as a symbol of Celtic perfection and declared his friend capable of intensities that he didn't exhibit. Lawrence came to Tregerthen at a time when Hocking found life on the farm both dull and confining. The war was making demands on all farmers, and with so many men in uniform there were fewer laborers to help with the harvest. Lawrence's arrival on the scene did much to make life bearable for William Henry. He was also flattered that a man as worldly and educated as Lawrence should want him as a close friend.

"My father left school when he was thirteen," said H. H. Hocking. "He was in the top standard at school, but when a boy reached thirteen, he was expected to work. The teacher at the school in Zennor came to see my grandfather. The teacher wanted Father to become a teacher too. But my grandfather was a sick man, and since Father was the oldest of seven children, he was expected to go into what was then called 'The Service'—to go live with a neighboring farm family and do the odd jobs. Do the dirty work, I presume. My grandfather had only fourteen acres, and when he died, in 1901, there was three years of rent owing. Since Father was the oldest, he became the tenant. The owner told Father to carry on as best he could. Father paid back the three years rent over a period of years, and in 1912, the landlord came to my father and said: 'Look here, my lad, you've done your best and you can have some more land.' So from then on Father had the neighboring farm as well. Father always said that it was through the landlord that he ever got as far as he did."

"William Henry would always think he had been done in,"

laughed P. O. Eddy. "I remember he once offered a cow to a man for thirty pounds, and the man said he would take her. Then William Henry was worried over the fact that he hadn't asked enough. I wouldn't have given twenty pounds for her. But that was William Henry for you. He did very well for himself."

"If you go right to the root of the matter with him," Lawrence wrote Dollie Radford, on October 11, 1916, when discussing his friend, "he is most marvellously understanding. He has thought deeply and bitterly." But Lawrence was beginning to doubt if it was right after all to ask his London friends to entertain the Cornishman. "He is a queer soul—I have got to know him quite well." Lawrence was impressed with the way the man brought his hand to his chest and intensely declared that there was something he wanted buried deep within himself, but would he ever be able to free the hidden hunger he felt? "There is something manly and independent about him—and something truly *Celtic* and unknown—something non-christian," wrote Lawrence, "non-European, but strangely beautiful and fair in spirit, unselfish."[10]

A St. Ives resident, who insisted on remaining anonymous, felt that William Henry was a "tyrant" as a husband and when imposing discipline on his children. "A very difficult man." When asked about this side of his father's nature, H. H. Hocking paused and said: "I suppose Father was an unusual man. He was very strict with us children. Mother didn't have anything to say about naming us. What Father said would be it. But he was a kindly man. Father was always very generous to beggars. The door at the farm would always be open to them, and they were never turned away. They would be fed and put up in the barn to sleep, after promising not to start fires. Father was that sort of man, and I think Lawrence felt that he could come to the farm and sit down by the fire."

William Henry had a reputation of disrupting the peaceful Zennor setting with pranks. The Hocking family remembered some of the tricks he played on people. There was one memorable night when William Henry whitewashed all the windows of a farmhouse and the occupants were late in rising the next morning. "Father enjoyed a practical joke," said H. H. Hocking. "I remember hearing people tell about Father and his friends dropping clods of earth on the heads of people who were passing by the church fence in Zennor, and tying the wheels of the traps to the frames outside the Tinners Arms. The old men would come out of the pub and get into their traps and roar at their horses: 'Gee-up, gee-up!' Of course the traps wouldn't move—the wheels were tied. Father and his friends would be off in a dark corner, laughing."

When asked why William Henry failed to answer Lawrence's letters, Stanley Hocking shook his head sadly and replied: "I don't remember—it was so long ago. I do know Lawrence wrote my brother several letters. But William Henry never answered a letter. He was no correspondent. Lawrence told my brother that he could have what things he liked in the cottage, but William Henry didn't do anything about it. The furniture was taken by a local auctioneer to St. Ives and was sold. There were a few sticks of furniture left at the farm; furniture Lawrence had brought down before he went away. These have been in the family ever since. I know Lawrence gave a tea set to one of my sisters and a coffee set to the other. Lawrence told William Henry he could have the piano, but my brother never got around to it. He couldn't be bothered."

"Father didn't get married until very late in life," said H. H. Hocking. "I believe he got married when he was thirty-five. In 1918." When the comment was made that this was the year after Lawrence left Cornwall, Hocking responded: "I think you will find that he got married after all his brothers and sisters were able to take care of themselves. He stayed on the farm at Tregerthen until 1934. Then he bought this farm (Trevega Walla, a neighboring farm). Uncle Stanley farmed Tregerthen." Had William Henry known Miss Eddy for long? "Oh yes," replied H. H. Hocking. "Father had known Mother for quite a while. They were all friends and neighbors in those days. But I believe Father and Mother really didn't become friendly until late in the war years."

"Father would sometimes speak of Lawrence," said Kitty Rogers. "But he never said much about him to us children. Lawrence was just an old friend who had lived nearby; someone Father had known in the past. I don't believe Father talked much about him to anyone. I do know that a few strangers came by to talk to Father about Lawrence—only a few—but Father's memory began to fail him rather early in life. He had trouble remembering much of what happened."

Shortly after Frieda's death, in New Mexico, William Henry was interviewed by a reporter. In the resulting article, published in *The Cornishman*, August 1956, Hocking claimed that Lawrence sometimes slept in one cottage and Frieda in the other, and he suggested that this was because "Lawrence might be engaged far into the night at his writing rather than there had been any quarrel between them."[11] If William Henry had been approached differently—even as late as 1956—perhaps some of the mystery of his relationship with Lawrence, that intense friendship, would have been explained. But it was not to be. William Henry died in 1962. He was buried beside his wife in the Zennor churchyard, behind the lovely stone chapel and in sight of the Tinners Arms.


## VII


Catherine Carswell came to visit the Lawrences on September 3. She was installed in the guest bedroom of the tower cottage, and they soon told her the story of Frieda wielding the stone dinner plate. This was her first stay with Lawrence and Frieda and it proved to be an agreeable one. Carswell, who had mostly praise for Lawrence as a person and talent, was not the kind to arouse Frieda's jealousy. There was an impersonality in her relations with him and she made no emotional demands. Catherine Carswell, who was to be one of Lawrence's most faithful defenders, received more than 170 letters from him and their correspondence continued until a few months before his death. The three went on a few walks together, but only a few as the weather turned stormy and cold. Frieda talked of going later in the month to see her children, and Lawrence had much to say about Dostoevsky and Murry's book.

During the visit, Carswell aroused Lawrence's puritanical wrath. She had retired to the tower cottage, and after having undressed for bed she remembered a book she had left in the living room of the Lawrences' cottage where they were still up. "I had brought no dressing-gown with me, but there seemed to me no impropriety in my costume—an ankle-length petticoat topped by a long-sleeved woolen vest! Lawrence, however, rebuked me. He disapproved, he said, of people appearing in their underclothes."[1]

In her book, *The Savage Pilgrimage,* Catherine Carswell carried further Lawrence's distaste for things he thought indecent. Carswell mentioned his hatred for the dog because of its public habits. In such matters Lawrence was no advocate of the natural. Nor was he "an apostle of the nude. I am sure," she wrote, "that he put down all our civilized indecencies—our coquetries as well as our callousness, our sophisticated desire to shock as well as our prurience—to a departure from natural reticence."[2] Carswell admitted that it might seem strange to all who had not considered the matter carefully, but she was convinced that only a man like Lawrence could have written *Lady Chatterley's Lover.*

Catherine Carswell and the Lawrences did the daily chores in their respective cottages without outside help, and the houseguest was delighted when Lawrence told her that she adapted better to the ways of cottage life than most of their friends in London. Carswell noticed that when Lawrence wasn't writing he would be working at something else with the same intensity he gave his literary pursuits. "Once he bought a gauze shawl of Paisley pattern for Frieda—cheaply, because it had a moth in it—and set himself to make it whole without delay by mending it himself. It took him two entire days, working well into the night, and allowing only the shortest intervals for his meals."[3] Carswell never saw Lawrence idle. He wasn't haunted by time or tortured by feelings of guilt; he seemed to work freely, eagerly and steadily until the task at hand was completed. She felt he had a tremendous capacity for enjoyment and work, and it wasn't in his character to harbor regrets and doubts. One day Lawrence might announce that he would never write another word, but this wasn't said in despair. It was more that he believed life to be greater than his books. Then a week later he would send out a new manuscript of poems or mention that he was typing the beginning of a new novel. Frequently, he burned stacks of manuscripts, and once at Tregerthen he nearly set the chimney on fire and worried the Hockings. There would always be a new thing to be written or some chore he could begin happily.

Giuseppe Orioli, who first met Lawrence in Cornwall and who became Lawrence's first publisher of *Lady Chatterley's Lover,* didn't share Carswell's high regard for the man. Orioli could never warm to him. The Italian bookseller found the fretful and distrustful part of Lawrence's personality too pronounced for a close relationship. Orioli objected to Lawrence's high opinion of his own work and to his feelings of not being sufficiently appreciated. "So far as such domestic arts were concerned he might have been a woman. He took more pride and pleasure in them than many women do; much more than his wife did."[4] Orioli described his business relations with the author as being more difficult than any he had ever experienced. Real friendship was impossible.

Catherine Carswell's stay at Tregerthen was cut short. Her husband, Don, unable to come and lonely at home, sent her a telegram to fetch her back. "Lawrence mocked at it all a little, but he had a way, not hurtful at all, of mocking gently at one. I remember our driving to the station at St. Ives and saying good-bye with the sense that my visit had been broken in half."[5]

Middleton Murry and Frederick Goodyear came to see Lawrence one day in mid-September while Frieda was in London. Goodyear, an old Oxford friend of Murry's and soon to die at the front, admired Lawrence's work and was eager to meet him. Lawrence was glad to see Murry, and the two got on well together throughout the visit. Lawrence showed them his vegetable patch. "It had been a garden once, but had long been abandoned; so William Henry, the neighbouring farmer, had told Lawrence he could have it, I think for a shilling a year."[6] ("That is nonsense," declared Stanley Hocking. "My brother was more generous than that!") Murry remembered Lawrence kneeling to part the parsnip leaves, and when Murry confessed that the roots were better than those he had raised at Mylor, Lawrence was pleased.

"Actually, he had two gardens," recalled Stanley Hocking. "He had quite a respectable patch in one of our potato fields, and another enclosed garden closer to his cottage. This wasn't much larger than an average-sized room. We had planted this little patch for generations. Mother called it her rhubarb garden. My older brothers used to plant several crowns of rhubarb there and covered them carefully during the winter with an old can that had the bottom knocked out. The rhubarb crowns had died out and the garden was empty. We told Lawrence he could use this patch. When he wasn't busy writing or helping us in the fields, he would be planting and growing things. Carrots, parsnips, peas, lettuce, parsley, and what he was most fond of, spinach and endive." Then Hocking added: "This was a rather difficult time for the Lawrences. He told us they had no money. He couldn't make any money out of his writings, and Frieda had to depend on any money she got from Germany, by way of Switzerland. We were given to understand that what she got there was very little. But life was pretty simple in those days. They got their chief necessities of life at the farm from mother. They could have butter, milk and eggs, an occasional chicken or rabbit. That would keep them from starving, and of course they always had a little money for groceries at the village shop in Zennor or in St. Ives. Bread, cheese and jam. So Lawrence grew his own vegetables."

Lawrence wrote Lady Ottoline Morrell on September 26. He hoped he could see her soon, when his novel was behind him. Could she come to them, or should they go to her for a while? Lawrence had heard that Bertrand Russell had been stripped of his lectureship at Trinity College and forbidden by the military authorities to enter any prohibited area—Russell had been making public statements advocating a new socialistic order, statements that were considered treasonable. Lawrence felt this wasn't the time to attack. Not when the country was at war. Russell should wait until the débâcle was over. "It is not martyrdom we seek." Lawrence wrote Ottoline. "I hate those who seek martyrdom. One wants victory. One wants this which *is*, shattered, and the chance to reconstruct according to one's heart's desire."[7]

Katherine Mansfield was smarting over something Lawrence had written to her—in a letter that was never found. He tried to explain on September 27: "You said I insulted you in my letter—well, I didn't. I can only say to you, as I said this time last year, when your brother died—there is a death to die, for us all. As for me, I am Lazarus sitting up very sick in his sepulchre."[8] Lawrence had another cold and was feeling shaky. But he and Frieda had finally made peace. It had been a struggle to the death. It was now time to build a new world and to make a new life—for them all.

Murry's visit had left Lawrence hopeful. Perhaps the two could meet and be friends again. In a letter to Murry, on October 11, he attempted to smooth over their differences and to predict a renewal of their relationship. When one was done with a person, one was done with the old in that person. This was what must be given up by them all to make room for the new. Lawrence believed they could be together again but warned that neither of them should state the time or terms. Then Lawrence wrote again of ending the "long and bloody fight" with Frieda. He considered it to be "the old Adam to be killed in me, the old Eve in her—then a new Adam and a new Eve."[9]

Frieda found Lawrence very ill and depressed when she returned from London. The landscape was dreary and there was so much dampness. She immediately took over as his nurse. It was an occupation in which she displayed a complete lack of talent. Frieda wasn't the person to attend the needs of someone ailing. Her clumsiness, carefree manner, and forgetfulness tortured him. Aldous Huxley, who was in Vence at the time of Lawrence's last illness, heard Lawrence weakly protesting when her concern for him increased her resolve to care for him. "Frieda, you have killed me," he said, aware of her failings.[10]

Lawrence wrote Amy Lowell on October 12. He wondered if his publisher, Duckworth, had sent her his two books published in June and July of 1916, the travel book, *Twilight in Italy*, and his collection of poems, *Amores*. She must tell him how she liked them. He wasn't happy with the Tregerthen weather. "The winter seems already to have come. The heather on the hills is dead, the bracken is dry and brown, and blowing away to nothingness. Already the fowls stand bunched-up motionless and disconsolate under stacks, out of the wind, the sky is all grey and moving."[11] Lawrence was feeling that way too.

On the last day of October, Lawrence was able to send his agent, J. B. Pinker, the last of *Women in Love*—all but the epilogue which he intended to write later, upon receiving the typescript from Pinker. He also sent along a story he had rewritten from manuscript—he called it "The Mortal Coil." Lawrence thought the story good but not destined for glory. It upset him to send Pinker another unmarketable piece of fiction. He was going to Italy when his stories sold. He claimed he was tired of being ill in England.

Robert Mountsier and Esther Andrews, two American journalists, had come to see him. Lawrence, who didn't have a high opinion of Americans as a rule, liked Mountsier and Andrews, and their visit rekindled his desire to go to America. His present mood was to leave England forever. America was a younger country, not as tired, and there was more freedom. "The world *is* bad," Lawrence wrote Koteliansky, "bad beyond bearing. So reject it, spit it out, trample on it, and have done with it in your soul." He felt the war couldn't go on for long, but while it lasted they were all trapped. They would have to leave England when it was over. "I tell you my Rananim, my Florida idea, was the true one. Only the *people* were wrong." He had finished with the Murrys. "So I have with Lady Ottoline and all the rest. And now I am glad and free."[12]

Frieda, who never had qualms in asking for assistance from those who were better off in the world, wrote Amy Lowell for money.

The American poet responded generously by sending a check for sixty pounds. Lawrence felt guilty because Frieda had asked for the money, but it would be accepted as a kindness, even if he were able to pay the money back. There was little generosity on earth, Lawrence wrote Lowell, and he would always remember her thoughtfulness. He was tired of being ill and without funds.

The harsh weather broke in mid-November, and for a few days Lawrence was in a better mood. On November 22, Lawrence and Frieda hired Tom Berryman to drive them to St. Ives. This was the first time in nine weeks that he had been away from Tregerthen. They visited Captain Short and his family, shopped for provisions, and drove back at dusk. "It was all gold, the West, when we drove home, all pure gold, with the rosy-purple host of the afterglow hovering above glistening. Far beneath we could see the tiny lights of the Scillies, glinting *so* tinily."[13]

That autumn had been a time of hibernation for Lawrence. He had wandered through his days, reading and cooking and looking at the sea. It was a kind of sleep in his life—"like the snakes and the dormice," he wrote Koteliansky. Then Lawrence recalled an incident at the spring where he got his water. Every day he or Frieda would take their pail and cross the lane in front of the cottage and follow the tiny footpath up the hill to where a well of cold spring water bubbled from the rocky earth. "I saw a most beautiful brindled adder, in the spring, coiled up asleep with her head on her shoulder," Lawrence wrote Koteliansky. "She did not hear me till I was very near. Then she must have felt my motion, for she lifted her head like a queen to look, then turned and moved slowly and with delicate pride into the bushes. She often comes into my mind again, and I think I see her asleep in the sun, like a Princess of the fairy world."[14]

This incident at the spring touched Lawrence deeply, and in his "The Reality of Peace" essays, written at Tregerthen, his experience of coming upon the adder began to take form: "If there is a serpent of secret and shameful desire in my soul, let me not beat it out of my consciousness with sticks." It would dwell in his subconscious where he couldn't touch it. "In its own being it has beauty and reality. Even my horror is a tribute to its reality. And I must admit the genuineness of my horror, accept it, and not exclude it from my understanding." Who is man to judge what must be on earth, and under the earth? Lawrence wondered. What right had man to destroy what had been created? "I must make my peace with the serpent of abhorrence that is within me." And the snake must take its place with honor. "Come then, brindled abhorrent one, you have your own being and your own righteousness, yes, and your own desirable beauty."[15]

But this wasn't the culmination. The final achievement had to wait until 1920, in Taormina, Sicily, when Lawrence recalled the adder in the spring at Tregerthen and wrote the best known of all his poems, "Snake."

Lawrence had gone for water—the scene: "On the day of Sicilian July, with Etna smoking." The princess had now become a "king in exile, uncrowned in the underworld," and voices in Lawrence said: "If you were a man/You would take a stick and break him now, and finish him off." But Lawrence confessed that he liked the snake, and felt honored "That he should seek my hospitality/From out the dark door of the secret earth." But as the venomous snake slowly drew up to ease himself "into/that horrid black hole," Lawrence picked up a log and threw it and the snake "writhed like lightning, and was gone"—leaving Lawrence to regret his act. "And so, I missed my chance with one of the lords/Of life./And I have something to expiate;/A pettiness."[16]

Lawrence's biographer, Harry T. Moore, didn't connect the letter to Koteliansky and the poem "Snake." Moore felt there was a possibility that Lawrence didn't remember the "Reality of Peace" passages when he wrote the poem three years later. "The prose is prophetic because it outlines an episode that was to occur later," wrote Moore, "and it is symbolic because in its very figurativeness it tells us what the episode meant to Lawrence."[17]

"In those days there was no water laid on at Higher Tregerthen," Stanley Hocking explained. "One had to go to the little spring, about a hundred yards up the hillside above Lawrence's cottage. There was a beaten path to the spring. One day Lawrence told me that he had had quite an experience while going for his water. I asked him what it could be, since there was little between his cottage and the spring. He told me there was an adder coiled up and lying in the spring. He said he stopped to look at her, and his first impulse was to kill her. 'But on second thought,' he said, 'could I kill her? Oh no! She looked so beautiful there. Then, as I approached,' he said, 'she raised her head and looked at me, and slid away into the grass with the grace and poise of a beautiful princess!' I had to laugh," said Hocking. "We don't admire adders that much. I remember my mother telling me that when she was a little girl of twelve and going to school, one of her schoolmates was bitten by an adder, and before they could get any medical help the child died. When I told Lawrence this, he didn't say anymore about the adder. But it's rather an unusual thing to find: an adder coiled up in your spring. You don't see that very often."

Lawrence's decision to have no more to do with Lady Ottoline Morrell was unexpected. She had done nothing to strain their friendship. Perhaps Lawrence was anticipating her reaction to *Women in Love*. There was enough in the book to lose the best of friends. Why he should have characterized her so cruelly, as Hermione Roddice, the unpleasant intellectual hostess, is difficult to explain. Perhaps he found her too dominating and no longer wanted her patronage. Lawrence wrote Catherine Carswell on November 21, saying that he was sending the typed manuscript of his novel which he had received from Pinker. He wanted Mrs. Carswell to read it and to make any corrections she thought necessary and to ask her husband, Don, if he thought any part of the book libelous. Philip Heseltine was Halliday, and the "Pussum" was a model called the "Puma." Lawrence insisted there was no one else taken from life. But on November 27, he was writing Carswell again. "I heard from Ottoline Morrell this morning, saying she hears she is the villainess of the new book." He had offered to send the manuscript to Ottoline, but he hoped she wouldn't want it. "Don't talk much about my novel will you? And above all don't give it to anybody to read but Don."[18]

Lady Ottoline was the daughter of Lieutenant General Arthur Cavendish-Bentinck and half-sister of the 6th Duke of Portland. She married Philip Morrell, a Member of Parliament, in 1902, and became one of the most celebrated women in London intellectual society. Many of the leading figures of the day were entertained at the Morrell's home at 44 Bedford Square, and later at Garsington Manor, near Oxford. It was in Bedford Square that Lawrence dined in August 1913, and after the appearance of his short stories, *The Prussian Officer*, in November 1914, she invited him frequently. The Morrells bought their country home and gave up their London residence when Lady Ottoline suffered a series of unexplained attacks of a nervous nature. She and Bertrand Russell began an affair in 1914, and though her husband knew about it, the arrangement lasted for two years. Morrell made his wife promise that she and Russell would never spend a night together. Her public appearances were sometimes grotesque; she would arrive heavily powdered and painted and with purple hair. She often accentuated her figure with huge hats and sweeping gowns.

Stephen Spender recalled seeing her on the streets carrying a shepherd's crook with several Pekingese dogs tied to it with ribbons. Her less generous visitors thought she had the face of a witch, and because of her red hair, Lawrence was reminded of Queen Elizabeth.

Lady Ottoline's interest in writers and painters was often looked upon as one of self-interest, but it was more a genuine desire on her part to assist and encourage the creative talents of her generation. Her generosity to the Lawrences was considerable. She opened her home to them, gave them presents, and when Lawrence was planning to escape England in 1915 she gave him thirty pounds for passage to America, a sum she couldn't really afford at the time. Frieda claimed that Garsington Manor and Lady Ottoline's social powers were very important to Lawrence.

It also meant a lot to Lawrence that Frieda was the daughter of a baron, but Lady Ottoline's lineage was even more impressive. He flirted with Ottoline, and she fussed over him. Frieda was intensely jealous and behaved badly at every opportunity. This caused strain between Lawrence and Frieda, and Lady Ottoline was quick to side with Lawrence. Mrs. Igor Vinogradoff, the Morrells' daughter, stated: "I think what happened when L. met my mother was that they both had strong sensitive passionate sympathetic personalities and they clicked." In *Women in Love*, Hermione (Ottoline) is in love with Birkin (Lawrence), and during a quarrel Hermione's hand closes "on a blue, beautiful ball of lapis lazuli that stood on her desk for a paperweight." Down on the head of the unsuspecting Birkin she brings "the ball of jewel stone with all her force"—a reenactment of the stone dinner plate that Frieda wielded at Tregerthen.[19] When asked to comment on any possible love affair between Lawrence and her mother, Mrs. Vinogradoff recalled her father saying that Frieda told him she wouldn't have minded L. and my mother having an ordinary affair— what she couldn't stand was all this 'soul-mush.' "[20]

One can imagine Lady Ottoline's reaction when she read what Lawrence had to say about her face in *Women in Love*. "There was something of the stupidity and the unenlightened self-esteem of a horse in it. 'She's got a horse-face,' Ursula said to herself, 'she runs between blinkers.' "[21] Ottoline was horrified and believed that Frieda had prompted Lawrence to render such a description. She felt it was a betrayal of their friendship and all she had done for Lawrence. Lady Ottoline never forgave him, and though she resumed correspondence with him again in 1928, she was always sensitive to the novel.

The Lawrences were still hearing from Frieda's family, and from what Lawrence could read into the attitude of Frieda's sisters, he believed that Germany wasn't ready for peace. Neither was England. He was convinced that the war was wrong and it was better for him to die than to violate his soul by taking part. It isolated him from his fellowman but he must do what his conscience directed. The Asquith government was being increasingly criticized in the newspapers for the slaughter of so many men in the Somme offensive, and Lawrence worried that a change in government might change the direction of the war with even more catastrophic consequences.

Catherine Carswell liked *Women in Love* and had only a few suggestions to make, such as giving a different shade to Gudrun's coat and changing the name of a minor character. Lawrence didn't think he would be going to London; it was impossible for him to get further than Penzance; he felt himself incapable of facing the world, yet he wanted to come. He guessed he would have to let Ottoline read the novel. He asked Carswell on December 2: "Do you think it would really hurt her—the Hermione? Would you be hurt, if there was some of you in Hermione? You see it isn't really her at all—only suggested by her." Then Lawrence hopefully added: "It is probable she will think Hermione has nothing to do with her."[22]

Mark Gertler had offered to lend the Lawrences money but there was no need. The sixty pounds from Amy Lowell had solved the money problem temporarily. His health had improved, he wrote Gertler, because he didn't work or bother to work. He was content to amuse himself like a child playing at work. "I have just made a 'pouffe'—a sort of floor cushion, square, and like a mound—and on the black cover, all round I have stitched a green field, then house, barns, haystacks, animals, man and woman, all in bright coloured stuffs—it looks very jolly and bright."[23]

All hopes for a new world seemed immediately dashed for Lawrence when word came in early December that the Asquith government had gone under and David Lloyd George was the new Prime Minister. This political turnover worried Lawrence. He considered Lloyd George to be incapable of leadership and the country would be steered into chaos. Herbert Asquith represented some of the decency of prewar England and the lingering love of liberty. But Lloyd George was "a clever little Welch *rat*," he wrote Amy Lowell on December 7, "absolutely dead at the core, sterile, barren, mechanical, capable only of rapid and acute mechanical movements." It was bad news for the country he loved. "God alone knows where he will land us: there will be a very big mess."[24]

The fall of the Asquith government was for Lawrence the beginning of a life and death struggle against giving in to the waves of patriotism sweeping the country. At all costs he felt that he must keep out of it. Isolating himself at Tregerthen now seemed impossible. He continued thinking of America as the best place where he could go to escape the inevitable disaster. He realized that he had no conscientious objections to war itself. It was still the spirit of the mob that alienated him. The same feelings he had when he went to Bodmin. He knew that men must fight and die—it was not this that left him bitter: it was again and again the mob spirit; that willingness in nearly every man around him to answer the call of death in the trenches.

Reports from Europe were not encouraging, and when he rode to Penzance with William Henry, Lawrence was gripped by the terrible wave of depression that swept through Cornwall. The Cornish farmers stood in little groups saying: "I'm afraid we're beaten. Them Germans are a wonderful nation, I'm afraid they're more than a match for us."[25] Lawrence, too, expected a national calamity. From his isolation, he tried to create the impression of not caring—that it didn't matter to him. But there was little consolation in the thought that a fearful disaster might strengthen the nation, and he felt as alienated as ever. More submarine chasers and destroyers were prowling back and forth in waters only a mile offshore at Tregerthen.

"Thank you for the little Dostoevsky book," Lawrence wrote Koteliansky on December 15. Lawrence had received *Pages from the Journal of an Author*, translated by Koteliansky and Middleton Murry, and published in December 1916. He had read only Murry's "Introduction" and Dostoevsky's "Dream of a Queer Fellow," and both gave him an unpleasant odor in the nostrils. Lawrence felt that Dostoevsky was "big and putrid." Then he turned on his former friend. "And Murry, *not being an artist*, but only a little ego, is a little muckspout, and there is an end of it." He had never claimed that Murry was honest. "I said we *had* liked him and therefore we still liked him. But one can mend one's ways. I have liked him and I don't like him any more. *Basta!*" Lawrence had been reading Cooper's *Deerslayer* and found it "exquisite." But "I don't want to hear you talk for a fortnight about Murry. Five minutes, then not for a moment more. Stink bores me, as well as oppresses me."[26]

Lawrence wrote Barbara Low to thank her for some newspapers she had sent. They made him ill, and he was now certain if one wanted to do something in England, one must avoid all connections with Cambridgeism, socialism and Fabianism. One must do things alone. He hadn't read Russell's *Principles of Social Reconstruction,* but he was sure it was bad. Lawrence was thinking of seeing his sister, Ada, in Ripley, for Christmas, but his elder sister, Emily, was coming down from Glasgow the 2nd week of January. Perhaps he would see them both at the same time and he could go to London for a week. He was lending his manuscript, *Women in Love,* to Esther Andrews, now in London. Low could go and see Andrews and finish reading the book. He would want to know what she thought of it.

The Lawrences had sent Dollie Radford a pendant of lapis lazuli for Christmas. In his letter to her on December 20, Lawrence wrote: "One hasn't the heart to make Christmas wishes. We *always* wish that better days would come: perhaps they will soon." The Lawrences would be staying at Tregerthen after all. "You know I keep saying I will come to London for a while. But something inside me won't let me. I am much better in health: much. But when I think of coming to London, a pressure comes on my heart, and I know it is impossible."[27]

December was a bitter conclusion to this year of quarrels, productivity, uncertain health, autumnal sleep, and war. Lawrence wrote Catherine Carswell on the same day he wrote Radford: "What an ugly farce Christmas is this year. Will anybody *dare* to sing carols, etc. Pah, it all stinks."[28] But with the sudden arrival of Robert Mountsier and Esther Andrews, he tried to shake his depression.

In "The Nightmare" chapter of *Kangaroo,* Lawrence vividly recalled Christmas Eve in their little cottage by the sea. Mountsier had brought a parcel of American dainties and Esther Andrews a big basket of fruit. They had decided to celebrate Christmas in spite of the pouring rain outside. Suddenly a hammering on the door. It was a St. Ives policeman who had come down the dark lane on his bicycle. He was there to inspect Mountsier's papers. More and more there were restrictions. The policeman questioned Mountsier carefully, apologized for the intrusion, and disappeared into the night. Lawrence caught himself wishing that he were an American too.

In a letter to Catherine Carswell on December 26, Lawrence wrote: "Christmas, thank goodness, is over. I hated its coming this year: I nearly hated even presents. I feel awfully downhearted—down altogether." He felt smothered and weary, as if he had been sent underground alive.  Then he asked Mrs. Carswell when the graves would open.  Mountsier and Miss Andrews were staying for the week. "Yesterday we had a party with the Hockings, which was jolly.  But my heart never felt so down in the dirt, as it does now."[29]

Stanley Hocking remembered the party.  "Yes, very plainly. Lawrence and Frieda and Robert Mountsier and Miss Andrews invited William Henry, my two sisters, Mabel and Mary, and me up to the tower for the Christmas night party which they were going to give and wanted us to join in.  So we went.  That was quite interesting. Quite interesting.  We all sat at a round table to begin with, Lawrence saying: 'Everybody here shall be equal tonight.'  In addition to the ordinary Christmas fare, Frieda produced a dish she called 'hot tamales.'  To me, they tasted like a superior sort of mincemeat, highly flavored with different spices, and served on a bay leaf.  It was very nice.  After supper we all sat around and sang different songs, and Frieda sang her German folk songs.  In those days I could play an accordion.  When Lawrence invited me to come up, he said: 'Don't forget to bring your accordion, Stanley.'  So I did.  I played and they sang, and as time went on, I had exhausted myself in playing all the simple little tunes I knew.  I ran short.  Lawrence said: 'Can't you play just one more, Stanley?'  I told him that I had played all that I could remember.  Then I thought and said: 'Yes, I can.  I can play just one more.'  I played the 'Merry Widow Waltz.'  Sad to say, Lawrence's face immediately fell.  He said to me: 'Please do not play that, Stanley!  I really cannot stand it!'  And I said: 'Why, what's the matter, Mr. Lawrence?'  'Oh,' he said, 'that reminds me of days gone by and people gone by and of everything that is sad.'  And then he added: 'Your instrument snorts like a prehistoric monster!' "

## VIII

Esther Andrews extended her stay with the Lawrences while Robert Mountsier left to arrange interviews with several London authors.  An unexpected interview awaited Mountsier upon his arrival in the city.  The Special Branch of the Metropolitan Police did the interrogating. Records show no trace of an investigation, but Mountsier wrote Lawrence that questions had been asked. Lawrence sensed disaster for England, and finding a noticeable increase of restrictions by the local authorities—it was forbidden to show lights from windows or to take photographs along the coastline—he felt more uneasy. With the new year upon him, he began to think about living in America. Mountsier and Andrews were planning to go back in March and the Lawrences wanted to accompany them.

His houseguests had increased his interest in American authors. Lawrence had already found Melville and Cooper to be impressive, and he admired Jean de Crevecoeur's *Letters from an American Farmer*. In a letter to Mountsier, on January 4, 1917, Lawrence listed the books he wanted sent down from London. The list included nearly every writer whose work would be discussed in his *Studies in Classic American Literature*. He wouldn't begin the essays until August of that year, and the final one, "Whitman," wouldn't be completed until February 1919, but his idea of developing a study on the transcendental elements in American literature was beginning to take shape.

"I didn't answer your letter about *Women in Love*," Lawrence wrote Lady Cynthia Asquith on January 8, "because it seems the book will not find a publisher in England at all. Indeed, nobody will print me nowadays, the public taste is averse to me. It is a nasty quandary. The books I have don't sell, so it's a bad look-out." He felt he couldn't go on living with the "miserable pittance" that his agent, Pinker, allowed him—"it is too insulting."[1]

Lawrence knew that their passports of November 1915 were no longer valid. Perhaps the authorities would allow them to leave England if there was sufficient reason. The need to earn money in America, the only country where his books were selling, seemed the best justification. But there was Frieda's birthplace to slow them up. Anything to do with Germany was a liability while Englishmen were dying; the more casualties at the front the uglier the mood at home. The Lawrences had enough money to get them to New York, and after arranging for the publication of *Women in Love* he and Frieda would go west, to California or the South Seas, and they would turn their backs on mankind. Many of his old associates were no longer eligible. William Henry would come. Mark Gertler was another possibility. But Gilbert and Mary Cannan were not sufficiently interested in such an adventure. Koteliansky he could count as one of the faithful. Never

Lady Ottoline and the Murrys—they were gone forever. "We shall all come to our Rananim before many years are out—only believe me— an Isle of the Blest," he wrote Koteliansky, "here on earth. But the first thing is to cut clear of the old world—burn one's boats: if only one could."[2]

Lawrence wrote Gordon Campbell, friend of the Murrys and a witness at Lawrence's wedding, asking help in getting their passports renewed. "I hope, in the long run, to find a place where one can live simply, apart from this civilization, on the Pacific, and have a few other people who are also at peace and happy, and live, and understand, and be *free*."[3] Campbell wasn't ready to renounce the world, though Lawrence was hopeful that this would be the case one day. Three days later, on January 25, Lawrence asked him for help again. Campbell, a barrister and then Assistant Controller in the Ministry of Munitions, might be able to use his influence. Lawrence explained that living "on the Pacific" didn't mean California but the Marquesas Islands, a place Lawrence became aware of by reading Herman Melville.

As a farewell to his old life, Lawrence was shaping some of his best unpublished poems into a book. He had written very few poems in Cornwall and this dry period would continue until 1920. But he was reading Whitman closely, and the Whitman influence would open his lines and release him from the conventional ties of Georgian poetry. Lawrence felt the poems he was gathering would be his last book of poems for many years to come. Most of them had been written four years before, during the months when Lawrence was completing the final draft of *Sons and Lovers*, in Italy, in late 1912 and early 1913. The collection was intimate and vital to him, and he was rather reluctant to submit the manuscript for publication. He was thinking of calling the book *Poems of a Married Man*, since the main theme of the poems was his marriage, the conflict of love and hate between husband and wife, but as he was never sure of titles the book was published in December 1917 by Chatto & Windus as *Look! We Have Come Through!* This led Bertrand Russell, still smarting over a quarrel with Lawrence to say: "They may have come through, but I don't see why I should look."[4]

Lawrence was pleased when the *English Review* accepted "Samson and Delilah" in January 1917. Perhaps he got the idea of the story from his long talks with Stanley Hocking's Uncle Henry. The fictional "Willie Nankervis" returns to "The Tinners' Rest" (The

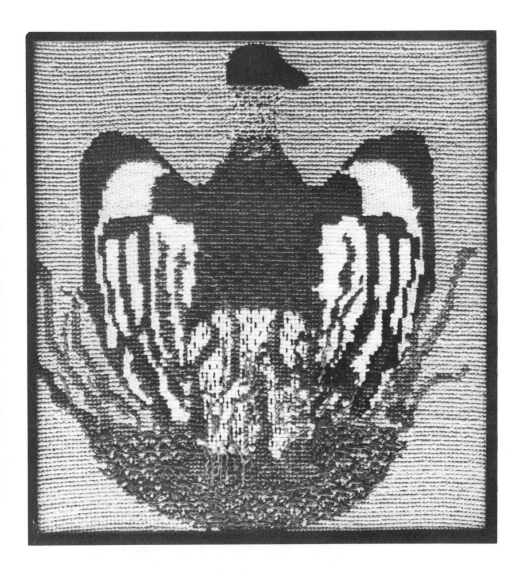

The phoenix tapestry Lawrence made for the Hockings

Tregerthen farm

Tower cottage

Bosigran Castle

Higher Tregerthen and lane to the farm

Tregerthen and the sea

Zennor village

William Henry Hocking

C. J. Stevens (left) and Stanley Hocking

Higher Tregerthen and Tregerthen farm

Lawrence's cottage

Tinners Arms), and his deserted wife who is the landlady of the pub doesn't recognize him. Nankervis had been to America for sixteen years and had worked in the mines at "Butte City." Uncle Henry didn't desert a wife, but he did work in the mines at Butte, Montana for a number of years, long enough to come back to Cornwall with a Willie Nankervis "Cornish-Yankee" accent.

Lawrence wrote J. B. Pinker, on January 29, that he was applying for passports immediately. Edward Marsh, editor of *Georgian Poetry* and longtime secretary to Winston Churchill, had been asked to advise. Marsh suggested that Lawrence make his reasons for wanting to leave the country as convincing as possible. Lawrence wrote Pinker: "I shall give 1. Ill-health 2. Failure to make any money at all over here. 3. Necessity to place short stories, and literary articles, and poems, and to arrange with a publisher the publication of *The Rainbow*, which is ready for press but has been deferred, and of the novel *Women in Love*."[5]

It was probably a mistake to have mentioned *The Rainbow* when applying to the passport office. Lawrence had often been scolded and seldom praised when his name came up in journals, and the appearance of *The Rainbow* caused a flurry of negative reviews. The first edition of the novel was published on September 30, 1915 by Methuen, Ltd. Though some of the criticism was because the book examined the sensations of physical love and how these sensations could and should be enjoyed by women as much as by men and also because he introduced a homosexual episode, the strongest criticism was directed at Lawrence's denunciations of industrialized England and the capitalistic system. War and nationality hadn't been examined along patriotic lines, and with England in the middle of its bloodiest war there were cries of outrage. James Douglas reviewed the novel in the *Star* and declared the book had "no right to exist." Douglas concluded his review by saying: "The young men who are dying for liberty are moral beings. They are the living repudiation of such impious denials of life as *The Rainbow*. The life they lay down is a lofty thing. It is not the thing that creeps and crawls in the novel."[6] A similar review appeared in *Sphere* the following day. Clement Shorter declared: "There is no form of viciousness or suggestiveness that is not reflected in these pages."[7] Solomon Eagle (J. C. Squires), in the *New Statesman*, asked if Lawrence was "under the spell of German psychologists."[8] Such criticism hastened the authorities into action. The police raided the warehouse where the books were stored, and Methuen, Ltd. was summoned before a London magistrate for bringing out a piece of indecent literature. The publisher was ordered to surrender all existing copies and to suppress all sales. This, soon after having been declared a bankrupt because of refusal and inability to pay law costs in Frieda's divorce case, was discouraging enough for Lawrence to threaten that he would never write another word he meant.

"I am afraid we are likely to get into trouble over D. H. Lawrence's new novel," Methuen wrote Pinker three days before publication, "and we hope he will moderate his broadmindedness in the next novel."[9] Methuen, Ltd. was quick to express regret for ever having published the book and to shift the blame on Lawrence when appearing before Sir John Dickinson. The magistrate was in full sympathy with the reviews written by Douglas and Shorter—it would have been difficult for him to have felt otherwise since his son had died in battle only six weeks earlier. Sir John was well aware that Lawrence was against the war, and he had been told that Lawrence had a German wife. The dedication of *The Rainbow*, to Else, Frieda's sister, a woman who was living in the enemy country, must have reenforced the magistrate's opinion that the book should be suppressed. It wasn't the best of times to make light of soldiers. Eyebrows were raised when Ursula Brangwen in *The Rainbow* teased her "best boy" for taking war seriously. "I hate soldiers, they are stiff and wooden."[10]

German submarines torpedoed two Norwegian merchant ships off Tregerthen. Stanley Hocking watched one of the vessels sink while the coast watchers saw the other go under with all crewmen lost. The skies had suddenly cleared, and Lawrence frequently sat in a sheltered part by the cliffs, away from the icy winds, reading and thinking about the move to America. But he was less hopeful that passport validation would be granted. Duckworth had turned down *Women in Love*, and Lady Ottoline was furious with him. "I told her it was her own fault," Lawrence wrote Catherine Carswell when Ottoline was brought up, "there was nothing to be in a frenzy over. So now I expect we are enemies for ever. I don't care. I don't care if every English person is my enemy—if they wish it, so be it."[11]

It was a bitter moment for Lawrence when word came that he and Frieda had been refused permission to leave England. He had little money, and with the suppression of *The Rainbow* and the unlikelihood of soon publishing *Women in Love*, his prospects were poor. In a letter to Lady Cynthia Asquith on February 12, telling her of the refusal to validate the passports, he declared: "You musn't think

I haven't cared about England. I have cared deeply and bitterly. But something is broken." He must now look for another world. Living in England was like taking up residency in a tomb. Then he asked Lady Cynthia: "Do you think I don't know what it is to be an Englishman?"[12]

On February 20, Lawrence wrote Pinker: "Really, the world has gone completely dotty! Hermione is not much more like Ottoline Morrell than Queen Victoria," and the "Breadalby" house belonging to Hermione Roddice was not the same as Lady Ottoline's "Garsington." But Lawrence did admit there was "a hint of her in the character of Hermione," but so were "a million women, if it comes to that." He assured his agent there were no grounds for a libel case in the book. "But it doesn't matter. It is no use trying to publish the novel in England in this state of affairs."[13] Lawrence felt there must be a complete change. His novel could wait until the war was over and the world looked upon things differently.

Lady Ottoline Morrell wasn't the only old friend who was characterized unfavorably in *Women in Love*. Philip Heseltine was another. The Lawrences had him as their houseguest while they were staying in J. D. Beresford's farmhouse in Padstow, Cornwall, long enough for Lawrence to like the young man, even if he did find Heseltine assertive. Cecil Gray was shocked when he read the novel in manuscript, in 1917, and found his close friend, Heseltine, depicted as Halliday, a pitifully weak and effeminate nonentity. Gray immediately told his friend, but Heseltine could "hardly have been prepared, however, for the extraordinarily venomous character of the libel," wrote Gray, "and there is no doubt he was deeply wounded by it."[14] The Halliday portrait of himself was too much for Heseltine, and he threatened the publisher, Martin Secker, with libel action while *Women in Love* was being published in 1921. Heseltine's case was questionable, but there already had been an attack on the American edition of the book in *John Bull* under the heading "A BOOK THE POLICE SHOULD BAN. Loathsome Study of Sex Depravity—Misleading Youth to Unspeakable Disaster."[15] Heseltine, who couldn't afford the costs of a court case at the time, requested that Lawrence make changes in the character Halliday for the English edition. Lawrence gave Halliday and the Soho model, Pussum, different shades of hair and sent the pages back. This wasn't enough for the injured party. The libel case continued, and the publisher eventually paid Heseltine five pounds and ten guineas costs.

Philip Heseltine appears in Chapter XXVIII of *Women in Love* as Halliday reading aloud a private letter from Birkin to a spiteful bunch of friends in London's Cafe Royal.  A barely disguised Katherine Mansfield snatches the letter from Halliday and marches out with great indignation.  "So plausibly is it told," observed Cecil Gray, "and so realistic and lifelike are the details, down even to the mock clerical voice in which Halliday reads out the letter," that Gray believed the incident to be factual until he came across a different version in Middleton Murry's *Reminiscences of D. H. Lawrence*.[16]  Murry claimed no letter had been read but poems from Lawrence's *Amores*.  Gray thought otherwise.  He knew his friend had a very high regard for Lawrence's poetry—even if Heseltine did use Lawrence's philosophy for other purposes.  Gray wrote Murry asking if Heseltine was the offender.  Murry was no longer sure but referred Gray to two eyewitnesses, one of whom, Koteliansky, was able to assure Gray that Heseltine hadn't been present.

Lawrence wanted to break away from Cornwall in late Frebruary, to visit Dollie Radford at her cottage in Berkshire and friends in London, but there seemed to be some unseen force which held him in Zennor.  He told himself that he would leave as soon as the spell lifted. The Foreign Office's refusal to validate their passports had stunned him.  He kept to his cottage and the farm, only occasionally walking to Zennor village for supplies and to chat with Katie Berryman in the shop.  There were signs of spring: the lambs were jumping in the field between his cottage and the farm, and the doves were cooing all day. The landscape was reviving from the long winter and Lawrence was waiting for signs of a new world.  He had been motionless too long at Tregerthen, rarely going to St. Ives or to Penzance with William Henry on market day.  Frieda was planning to visit London in March. Perhaps he would accompany her.

The disappointment of not being permitted to leave for America didn't damage his magnificent ability to produce new work.  He had completed seven short essays called "The Reality of Peace," and he was proud of them.  They represented an important beginning for him.  He felt it was time to bring new life into the world.  He immediately sent the work to Catherine Carswell and told her they must "all think *hard* about their publication."[17]  He had written Austin Harrison of the *English Review*.  Lawrence asked Carswell if she thought the magazine would publish them.  The essays weren't about the end of hostilities and peace between Germany and England.  There was another kind of peace. He was directing his attention to a more timeless issue. The peace to be found in the soul.

With the coming of spring and sunnier days, Lawrence began to increase the two garden plots by his cottage. He was worried about a shortage of food. He wrote Koteliansky asking for a book on gardening—*Culture of Profitable Vegetables in Small Gardens.* Then Lawrence commented on the latest gossip concerning old friends. Mark Gertler was unhappy because Dora Carrington wouldn't return his intense love—she was about to desert Gertler for Lytton Strachey. And the sad news of Gilbert Cannan: he had suffered a nervous breakdown, his marriage to Mary Ansell Cannan was disintegrating because he had a mistress, and Cannan also had got his wife's maid pregnant. Lawrence asked for more news from London, and had Koteliansky heard from Murry? "I have not heard from either of them for many months, which is as it should be. I have really a disillusion from them."[18]

Lawrence received five pounds from Amy Lowell for his poem "Terra Nuova," later to be called "New Heaven and Earth." The poem was to appear in Lowell's *Some Imagist Poets: An Annual Anthology.* Lawrence wasn't an imagist, nor did he consider himself to be one, but the money was accepted gladly. Frieda spent a few days in London— "chasing her children," as Lawrence was always quick to explain. An invisible force still held him in Zennor. The Lloyd George government had just been given the power to recall for examination all men who had previously been rejected on any grounds. The prospect of having to stand naked before the doctors in Bodmin again worried him. He would rather go to prison than serve in the military. "The Reality of Peace" essays weren't as meaningful to the Carswells as he had hoped and this disappointed him, but the *English Review* was going to publish some of them. Frieda had visited Mark Gertler, and Lawrence wrote to the young painter on April 1. Koteliansky had Lawrence's *Women in Love* manuscript and Gertler could borrow it to read. "And then, please tell me how much likeness you can see between Hermione and the Ott. The Ott is really too disgusting, with her threat of legal proceeding, etc. She is really contemptible. We have flattered her above all bounds, in attending to her at all."[19]

Esther Andrews came down from London to visit the Lawrences unexpectedly. Robert Mountsier had sailed back to New York alone, and she was feeling stranded and miserable. Lawrence had promised to meet his two sisters at the younger sister's home in Derbyshire, and with Esther Andrews as company for Frieda, Lawrence also decided to brave the chaos of London and to spend a week with friends there. Surprisingly, one of the friends he wanted to see again was Middleton Murry. He hoped Murry was well, and would Murry let him know at his sister's address in Derbyshire?

Lawrence fell ill with a stomach disorder while visiting Koteliansky, but after a few days in bed he had recovered enough to go see Dollie Radford at her Hermitage cottage in Berkshire. Dr. Muriel Radford, wife of Dr. Maitland Radford, recalled: "Dollie was fond of Lawrence, and he of her. It was said, I believe, of him that he was at his best in the country, but for the day or two he was with us he seemed to me a sad man; I cannot remember what we talked about. Whilst we were walking in the woods he stopped to watch a jay in flight and delighted in the color on its wings. The cottage was candle-and-lamp-lit; Lawrence would not allow three candles to be alight at the same moment; he said it brought bad luck."[20] From the cottage in Hermitage, Lawrence returned to Cornwall on April 27 to find Frieda ill. He thought it was some inflammation of the bowels and quickly wrote a note asking Dr. John Dyer Rice, the Hockings' doctor from St. Ives, to stop by and to examine her. Dr. Rice found Frieda to have had ptomaine poisoning which had progressed to colitis. Koumiss was prescribed and her condition slowly improved.

Another problem for Frieda at this time, according to Mabel Dodge Luhan in her *Lorenzo in Taos*, was Miss Andrews. Mrs. Luhan claimed that Frieda told her that for the first time Lawrence had been "unfaithful." Frieda "with a kind of bitter triumph" had said "it was unsuccessful." Catherine Carswell insisted that Mrs. Luhan's account was "both misleading and incorrect." Mrs. Carswell had heard the story from both Frieda and Lawrence. The girl "was unhappy" from the Mountsier experience, "and in the strength of her unhappiness could not resist attaching herself to Lawrence and trying to match her strength against Frieda's—disastrously to herself." Mrs. Luhan claimed Frieda sensed mischief and "showed the girl to the door."[21]

Catherine Carswell was always one to see the better side of Lawrence in everything. Her account of him was given more attention than what Mabel Dodge Luhan had to say in her *Lorenzo in Taos*. Albert Perry, in his book *Garrets and Pretenders*, called Luhan's book "*Lorenzo in Chaos*." Mrs. Luhan's critics thought her off balance when she recalled her associations with Lawrence in New Mexico, and she did seem to have a way of not getting the full confidence of her viewers—

as if she deliberately set out to distort whatever happened by painting the plain truth with the brightest of colors.

Mabel Ganson Evans Dodge Sterne Luhan was an only child from a wealthy banking family in Buffalo, New York. She had four husbands and lived for many years in Europe. Well-known as a patroness of the arts, she settled in Taos, New Mexico and became a champion of local Indian affairs. Her reason for coaxing Lawrence to Taos was to get him to write about the Indians and to call attention to their financial and spiritual plight. She also wanted Lawrence for herself, not romantically, but more to become emotionally involved with him and to usurp his gifts. Lawrence described her to his mother-in-law, Frau Baronin von Richthofen, as one who "wants to be a witch and at the same time a Mary of Bethany at Jesus's feet—a big, white crow, a cooing raven of ill-omen, a little buffalo."[22]

Mabel Dodge Luhan introduced an anonymous memoir in her *Lorenzo in Taos*, a description of Lawrence and Frieda at Tregerthen. The memoir had been sent to Luhan while she was writing her book. The anonymous reporter, probably Esther Andrews—if it wasn't Luhan at her imaginative best—described Lawrence as he appeared to her while she was in Cornwall. She referred to his mother complex which prompted him to write *Sons and Lovers*. The first time the reporter had seen Lawrence, he had talked steadily all afternoon, brilliantly and frankly. She thought *Women in Love* was his "final philosophy." She also pointed out how quickly he could be angered by criticism, and how he had quarreled with all his friends. Yet they were willing "to come back for the same treatment again and again." There was a sunnier side to the man. "The peasants around where he lived in Cornwall adored him, blindly. They looked upon him as the new Messiah come to lead the world out of the dark into a light that they couldn't understand, but which they had infinite faith in, simply because he was he." ("My God!" said Stanley Hocking. "I should think that is cutting things very thick indeed! We *never* looked upon Lawrence as a messiah. All this is damned nonsense!") Frieda was described as a big German woman with a sweet disposition, "who, as the daughter of a Prussian officer, never knew anything but luxury" while growing up. She was "impractical" in her housework and had "an expansive child-nature." People were always visiting Lawrence, and though he hated this he was always very patient with his callers.[23]

Lawrence wrote to Middleton Murry again on May 5. He

guessed that his former associate preferred not to acknowledge his previous message. Frieda was still unwell but she was improving. Heseltine had shown up at the Tinners Arms to Lawrence's distress. He had heard that Heseltine was going to live in a small bungalow on the moors, beyond Zennor, on the road to Penzance. He no longer liked the young man, and the friendly feelings he once had for him would never return. There were no changes at the farm—only "little domestic upheavals which are too long to write." He had gone to Penzance the day before—it was William Henry's market day. "All the Cornish farmers are filled with the sense of inevitable disaster: talk freely of the end of the world.—I give it all up. One can only stand far off, and watch—or not watch. Heaven knows what the end will be."[24]

## IX

"Lawrence had a different way of binding the sheaves," said Stanley Hocking when recalling the summer of 1917. "He would bind them with what we would call a Midland knot. Our sheaves had to stand quite a bit of handling, and we had to bind them in a certain manner. Very tightly and very efficiently. Now Lawrence would bind them all right—they were bound by straw. Just a little wisp of straw you would pull out with your hand and twist and tack under. But he had a different method of making the knot, and I must admit that his sheaves wouldn't stand much handling. In the winter the sheaves had to be pulled out from the rick and carried through the barn to feed the cattle. This meant several more handlings. And if those sheaves weren't done properly, they would all come adrift. We could always tell at a glance: 'Oh, this is one of Lawrence's sheaves here!' "

Lawrence was spending more time with William Henry and the Hockings. He seemed to be drifting away from Frieda, even away from himself as he helped with the harvest. He was writing less now, and though he still kept in contact with Gray the center of his life was the farm.

"He couldn't handle the fork in the orthodox manner that we stout country farmers did," replied Stanley Hocking when asked if Lawrence knew much about farming. "We would take the fork, plunge it in, and fling the hay or corn up. But Lawrence had the inclination to handle the fork more like a woman. Sometimes he hardly knew which hand to put forward first. In handling a fork, you're either left- or right-handed. Lawrence would try to use the fork both ways."

Did they hire Lawrence to work on the farm? The question surprised Stanley Hocking. "Of course we never hired him. He wouldn't condescend to become a farm laborer! But he always would say: 'I want to be one of you. I want to labor in the fields and help you with the harvest. Like one of you.' He loved coming down and doing what he could. I know he used to come and ask: 'Well, what are we going to do today?' "

And what was Lawrence's favorite work on the farm? "Definitely harvesting," replied Stanley Hocking. "Lawrence loved harvesting. It was always done in beautiful weather. The sun was shining and it was warm and comfortable. Frieda would sometimes come down and help too. Lawrence and Frieda were delighted when my sisters brought out croust in the afternoon. Croust is a Cornish word. I don't think you'll find it in the Oxford Dictionary. It means tea served out of doors in the afternoon."

Recalling this time in "The Nightmare" chapter of *Kangaroo*, Lawrence wrote that the neighbors were jealous of the Hockings. " 'Buryan (Hocking) gets his labour cheap. He'd never have got his hay in but for Mr. Somers,' (Mr. Lawrence) they said. And that was another reason for wishing to remove Richard Lovat. (D. H.) Work went like steam when he was on Trendrinnan (Tregerthen) farm, and he was too thick with the Buryans."[1]

"That's a good one," laughed Stanley Hocking when hearing the quote read from *Kangaroo*. "We had another workman besides Lawrence, and Lawrence was only considered a boy compared to this other workman. 'Work went like steam' not because Lawrence was there. There were many days when he wasn't there, and work went on as usual. Lawrence only came to suit himself—providing the weather was suitable, and if he didn't get tired. But he always knew what to do if he got tired. He would make some excuse, pack up, and go up the lane. And if it was pouring rain, you wouldn't see him for a week. Lawrence wasn't very strong. Not strong enough to hold a sheep that would probably weigh one hundred and fifty to one hundred and eighty pounds. Speaking of sheep, I remember Lawrence was quite interested in sheep shearing. It always amused him. He would say: 'They look so naked, don't they!' But as a workman, Lawrence could do the little—what shall I say?—the insignificant jobs in the fields and on the rick. He could get on the rick and hand the hay from the pitcher to William Henry who was building the rick. He loved that. He could do that. He could do that better than pitching off a load. It's no joke, pitching off a load of hay from a wagon. That's hard work. But as soon as hay is taken from a wagon and placed on a rick, the hay is loose. Lawrence could hand loose hay or sheaves to the builder. A boy of eleven can do that. I've pitched many a load to Lawrence."

"Lawrence thought he was helping on the farm," said H. H. Hocking, "but he wasn't really experienced enough to do much. And to be honest, Lawrence wasn't all that strong. He was a frail man. I don't think his work suited Father. I just think that Father accepted the fact that what Lawrence was doing would do. After all, he was Father's friend, and he enjoyed Father's company. I believe Lawrence would be putting into words what he had learned during those three or four days. There wasn't any dependable arrangement made. I think Lawrence came down when he felt like it."

"William Henry never said much about Lawrence helping on the farm," Arthur Eddy recalled. "He said that Lawrence used to come down and talk with him. But any of these city people who come down to a farm to help will think they are doing a big thing. Yes, they always think they are doing a big job."

"John Thomas was a year or two older than Somers," wrote Lawrence in *Kangaroo*, "and at this time his dearest friend." He so much liked being with his farm friend, the two lying on the heather and talking while the others were coming with the wain. "Somers loved these people. He loved the sensitiveness of their intelligence. They were not educated. But they had an endless curiosity about the world, and an endless interest in what was right." So often they questioned him. " 'Now do you think it's right, Mr. Somers?' The times that Somers heard that question, from the girls, from Arthur (Stanley), from John Thomas."[2]

"So he said we were not educated, did he?" said Stanley Hocking with noticeable irritation. "That's a sharp one, isn't it? What does an education do for you? In those days, going to college wouldn't have been an advantage in getting a living out of the soil as a Cornish farmer. You've got to be brought up into it. You've got to know what each individual field is capable of growing, and what it takes for attention to make things grow. Otherwise, you would be a failure. And this knowledge comes to you only with years of experience. I dare say we asked him a lot of questions. But I think we were happier in our way of life by not having contact with the outside world. The outside world didn't make Lawrence happier than we were. He might have seen too much of the ways of the world. Too much for his own good."

"But he loved being with us," Stanley Hocking continued. "He used to sit there in the kitchen. There was a big table a dozen people could sit around. The old dresser was on the right side, and a little seat by the old Cornish slab. Lawrence was very fond of sitting on this little seat, especially when Mother was frying potatoes. As soon as the potatoes were ready, he'd be picking them out from the pan, one or two at a time, little potato slices, and putting them in his mouth, saying: 'These are lovely, Mrs. Hocking! You are the best cook in the whole world!' Poor old Lawrence, I can see him doing that now. He really enjoyed Mother's cooking. Very much. Mother would often cook a joint of beef or a small chicken for them on Sundays. This used to please them. In those days, there was only a small oil stove for a cooking arrangement in their cottage. There wasn't a Cornish slab. If you had a Cornish slab or range, there would be an oven at the side, but with their oil stove the Lawrences had only a flame and you had to watch it. If the flame got too high, the stove would smoke."

Then Hocking paused, recalling another incident. "I know he used to give our sheep dog, Nell, tidbits from his table, until he discovered her going through the door one day with his weekly joint of beef. He called her and called her, but she wouldn't come back. So the next day he set a mousetrap with cheese. Nell came in as usual and started sniffing around the table. Off went the mousetrap and hit her on the nose! He said Nell went through the door like a streak of lightning! She never came back to Lawrence's cottage after that."

Signor Raul Mirenda, Lawrence's landlord at Villa Mirenda in Florence, recalled a similar incident which occurred in 1926. Lawrence had prepared some lamb for roasting and had left it on a table in his dining room while he went out on the balcony on some other task. A peasant's dog entered the house and fled with the roast. Lawrence tried to catch the animal but the chase proved useless. " 'Today Geppurillo (that was the name of the dog) will eat better than we,' " Lawrence declared good-humouredly."[3] Stanley Hocking hadn't read Edward Nehls' *D. H. Lawrence: A Composite Biography* in which the Mirenda contribution appeared. The similarity of the two accounts can be called a coincidence.

Lawrence did find domestic creatures distasteful at times. The episode of Lawrence's dog, Bibbles, as recalled by Knud Merrild in his book *A Poet and Two Painters,* is a frightening story indeed, and there have been many comments on the incident. Those who admire Lawrence refuse to believe it, and those who detest the man are quick to accept the story as another example of his unstable behavior and meanness. Merrild and a fellow Danish painter spent the winter of 1922-1923 near Lawrence in New Mexico. Lawrence befriended the dog and he even made her the heroine in one of his animal poems in *Birds, Beasts and Flowers.* The new master expected absolute loyalty from Bibbles. He in return would protect her from the ranch dogs that were after her now she was in heat. But Bibbles ran off with the first passing ranch dog, and when she returned she was soundly whipped by Lawrence. Again, she ran away, this time out of fear, and when she came back to the ranch she went to the Danes' cabin. Lawrence descended upon them all, pale, and trembling with rage. "So there you are you dirty, false little bitch!" He rushed after her, upsetting tables and chairs, and through the door into the deep snow they both went. He caught her, kicked her, and would have killed her if Merrild hadn't rushed between them. Lawrence did forgive Merrild and Bibbles in the end. He baked some delicious bread and cake for the Danes the next day, and several days later Bibbles came back to Lawrence's house and jumped on his bed as she had done in the past.

"I do know that Lawrence liked animals," said Stanley Hocking when hearing the story about Bibbles. "He was very fond of Blossoms, our big cart horse. Blossoms stood seventeen hands high and weighed about a ton. He used to ride her around the fields in his spare time. Lawrence always had a turn for things. I remember he would say: 'Gee-up, gee-up, my beautiful Blossoms, you are my moving mountain!' And off they would go."

"Lawrence was rather interested in me," Stanley Hocking remembered. "He thought it was a pity that I left school at fourteen. He told me: 'You could have done better, my boy.' I told him it was a matter of chance. It wasn't a question of going out into the world and looking for a job. My job was waiting for me on the farm. There was always something to do. We had lots of cattle and sheep to look after in those days. So Lawrence offered to teach me French. He also showed me how to play chess and bridge. He was a good teacher and very patient. Just before he left Tregerthen, I remember him telling me: 'I think you are a very good pupil, Stanley.' He would give me certain little lessons, and he was always telling me that certain words in English did not translate."

"It had its charm for Harriet," (Frieda) Lawrence wrote in *Kangaroo*, "this aspect of him—careless, rather reckless, in old clothes and an old battered hat."[4]

"I remember that very well indeed," interrupted Stanley Hocking. "When he came into the fields to help us, he would dress in anything. Old shoes. Old trousers. An old battered hat. He said he wanted to look like one of us. But when he went to St. Ives, I remember he had a decent gray suit."

Stanley Hocking was shocked when asked: If you crept up behind Lawrence and *suddenly* placed your hand on his shoulder, how do you think he would react? "Oh my! Oh gosh! That would be the wrong thing to do with Lawrence. I wouldn't like to do that! He would probably take it as an insult. He wasn't one who was going to be manhandled by anyone. If Frieda found fault with him about anything, he would immediately fly into a rage. He had a quick temper, I must admit. He didn't like to be criticized."

And Frieda? Hocking answered after a sip of wine. "Frieda wasn't the philosopher he was. She was gayer and liked to see the funny side of life. I know one day she said to me, while looking at the old sow: 'I'm sure you farmers must make a fortune. Take one of your old sows, for instance. She has dozens and dozens of little pigs every year!' It was so funny hearing these people make their little remarks. Lawrence, at times, was quite lighthearted and could see the fun in anything too. But on other days he would be depressed, as if something was worrying him. What that was we never knew."

Frieda would sometimes come to the farm and work in the fields with the Hockings, but she could never warm to their ways. She never let them forget that she was the daughter of a German baron— a role she loved to play. Frieda often mentioned her background with pride, and her sister, Else, would laugh at her for boasting about their pedigree. Her branch of the von Richthofen family was poor. There were no dowries for the von Richthofen girls, and her father didn't improve matters with his gambling. But Lawrence was impressed. He had written letters to friends upon coroneted stationery, proudly explaining that his father-in-law was a baron. The family wasn't of ancient nobility; the title went back only two and a half centuries. But a baroness was a baroness. Lawrence often associated with women who had titles: Lady Ottoline Morrell, Lady Cynthia Asquith, the Honourable Dorothy Brett. He once confessed to Lady Ottoline that he would have given much to be an aristocrat.

"Now look here," said Stanley Hocking, "this reminds me of a rather amusing remark that our workman made about Frieda and Lawrence. This workman was a bit of a lad and he had a droll wit. I remember we all had our tea in the harvest field one day, and after Frieda and Lawrence had gone home, this old boy said to me and William Henry: 'Where in the hell did she find him? I should think that she must have found him in a *Lucky Bag*!' In those days we would go to a shop and buy a halfpenny *Lucky Bag*. A little bag made up and containing two or three sweets and maybe a thimble or a squeaker. He did have a rather squeaky voice. Even Lawrence felt that Frieda was superior to him. She had a different manner, and she talked very nicely. She didn't come in and sit down the way he did in the evening. When she came down for the milk you could guess that Lawrence was rather unwell. She would go back up the lane to give him his supper. Frieda couldn't be considered one of us the way Lawrence was. I must say that. We had to admit she lived in a different world from us. A German baroness is not going to consider herself on the same level as an ordinary Cornish farm girl or wife. And her father was a German baron. There will always be that barrier. Call it a social barrier, if you will, but it will always be there. Mind you, Frieda might have felt quite a bit isolated. She was a stranger in a strange land, and there was no one of her class in the locality for her to be really friendly with. But Frieda wasn't class-conscious. Not as much as we were. Particularly, my mother and sisters. They felt the difference, I know. Women have a natural aptitude for feeling this sort of thing. I can remember one of my sisters saying: 'She's more of a lady than he is.' We loved for Frieda to come down in the fields, but my sisters were a bit uneasy. My sisters had the feeling that Mrs. Lawrence was a lady. I heard Frieda say to Mother one day when Lawrence was looking particularly ragged and sweaty: 'Lorenzo looks more like one of you every day. I don't know what I'm going to do with him!' "

"Lawrence wasn't much for dressing," Stanley Hocking remembered. "But Frieda always dressed very nicely. I saw her once or twice in a Bavarian costume which was nice. I think her hat was red and white with a wide brim. Whether or not it was the Nelson-style hat, I can't remember. But her dress and bodice were very picturesque. A sort of laced-up affair in front with a black skirt and a tiny little apron worked with flowers."

When asked to recall more about Frieda, Hocking responded with a smile: "Frieda had a piano in the cottage and she used to play it a bit. It was an old one, but it sounded rather well. She could play nicely. But my accordion would not harmonize with Frieda's playing at all." Did she have an accent? "Frieda spoke fairly good English," said Hocking. "But I could detect what I would call an accent when she pronounced certain words. Do you recall that song, 'Row your Boat'? Well, Frieda could sing it very nicely, but she would always sing: 'Woe, woe your boat.' "

Ivor Short's impression differed from Stanley Hocking's. "I never noticed a trace of an accent at all. If she had one, I would have picked it up at once." And how did Lawrence strike one as a person? "The same as I strike you," replied Short. "There was nothing extraordinary about him. He used to tell me about his upbringing. He had nothing at all—he was just a miner's son. He told me about his father and the mines. Lawrence had a rotten life as a boy, and how a miner's son got where he did is a mystery. Lawrence never bothered anybody. He was docile. He wouldn't say boo to a goose. He wasn't antagonistic and bad-tempered. Put it this way, he was an Englishman."

## X

With Esther Andrews gone, Lawrence attended a convalescing Frieda. He was still feeling the effects of his illness at Koteliansky's but he was recovering. Much to Lawrence's relief, Heseltine was keeping out of sight; he had seen "little or nothing" of him since the young composer had moved into the Trewey Consolidated bungalow on the Penzance road. Lawrence was busy cutting Blackthorn and gorse in order to keep Hockings' lambs from devastating his garden. "I loathe lambs," he wrote Koteliansky, "those symbols of Christian meekness. They are the stupidest, most persistent, greediest little beasts in the whole animal kingdom. Really, I suspect Jesus of having had *very little* to do with sheep, that he could call himself the Lamb of God. I would truly rather be the little pig of God, the little pigs are infinitely gayer and more delicate in soul."[1] The garden was thriving, but the Hockings' lambs had raided his broad beans.

"I don't see how our lambs could have entered Lawrence's garden," said Stanley Hocking. "We always were very particular with our fences at Tregerthen." When asked to explain what possibly could have led Lawrence to observe in "The Reality of Peace," that when sheep get into a garden they munch on roses with little appetite but hungrily consume the cabbages, Stanley Hocking, troubled by the thought, paused for a moment. "Lawrence could make rather snippy remarks at anything. I remember once we were watching the lambs playing on the tops of big rocks in the field and having races together. He used to like that. He said to me one day while he was watching them: 'It's all very well to see the dear little lambs playing and gamboling, but what are they born for? Only for the cruel butcher's knife. Futile it all is,' he said. 'Every birth means a death. Therefore all life is futile.' "

S. S. Koteliansky sent a telegram requesting that Lawrence work with him on the Russian translation of a Gorki paper. Koteliansky felt his English too faulty to carry him through a successful work of translation without assistance. This call for help eventually led to a collaboration on Leo Shestov's *All Things are Possible*, published by Martin Secker in 1920, and Dostoevsky's *The Grand Inquisitor* and other works. John Middleton Murry worked with Koteliansky on several translations before Lawrence agreed to assist. But Lawrence's name never appeared on any of these books. He felt it would be damaging to his career as a creative writer. *All Things are Possible* was heavily revised by Lawrence; so much so that Lawrence rewrote the entire translation in his own handwriting.

On May 23, Lawrence asked Murry if he would be going to Mylor that summer, and would he stop by to visit them at Tregerthen? Murry was working at the War Office in London. Lawrence had taken to his bed with another cold but was "reviving like a plant after rain." It had been a year since the Spanish ship *Manu* had been wrecked off Tregerthen. There had been many changes. Lawrence had no writing news. "Philosophy interests me most now—not novels or stories." He was weary of man, and one couldn't have fiction without people. He again brought up their old relationship. "You shouldn't say you love me. You disliked me intensely when you were here, and also at Mylor.

—But why should we hate or love?"[2] They were two different persons and had to be themselves separately.

"Lawrence was always writing," said Stanley Hocking, "even when philosophy interested him. If he was helping us in the fields and something occurred to him, he would drop whatever he was doing immediately and go in and write for the next two or three hours. He had a typewriter, and after he had left a nearby field we would sometimes hear the typewriter tapping away. But he never told us much about his writings. The only clue I got of publishers refusing his work was through Frieda. She mentioned it quite often. She thought his writings were too much philosophy. Lawrence could always find something to write about. But the trouble with him was that he couldn't dispose of his work. He couldn't make any money out of it. I do know that he wrote some articles for the *English Review*. They were called 'The Reality of Peace.' He gave us one or two copies of these. He was rather pleased that they had been accepted. I believe Lawrence was writing a lot of articles in those days. They were nearly all returned as not quite good enough for publication, and when they did come back they were very often burned. I was there one day when Frieda threw a bunch of them on the fire and burned them in front of him." When asked what Lawrence's reactions were, Hocking recalled: "Lawrence was wild. Frieda told him off. I remember her saying: 'There you are, Lorenzo, they've all come back again! They are all philosophy and nobody wants them!' Into the fire they went. What they were I never knew. He was very annoyed with her."

Did Lawrence ever talk about poetry? "A bit," said Stanley Hocking, "but of course I don't recall what he said about it. I do remember him telling me that he was rather keen on making poems himself. And he did quote a few lines of Shelley's verses to me one day by Wicca Pool. In fact, it was in August 1917, just before he went away. I remember this distinctly. Wicca Pool was down by the cliffs where Lawrence and Frieda went swimming. They went down there quite often during the summer months of June, July and August. Sometimes Lawrence would go there alone. I had been to see if the young cattle and sheep were all right on this particular day in August when Lawrence came along. He remarked on what a beautiful day it was. The sun was shining very brilliantly, without a cloud in the sky, and the sea was very blue. He said to me: 'If we look about us, Stanley, here are all the things that Shelley wrote in his poem about the ocean. Do you happen to know the poem?' I said: 'I'm afraid I don't know any of

Shelley's poems at the moment.' Then Lawrence asked me if I would like to hear him recite a few verses. I said: 'Yes, go ahead if you like.' So he recited several verses to me."

A newcomer turned up at the Tinners Arms and soon rented a house on the coast near Pendeen called Bosigran Castle. It was then a ramshackle, two-story structure with windows facing the sea and standing alone near the cliffs where the lonely moors sloped to the surf by an abandoned tin mine. The place was three miles from Zennor village and located in a strategic area where German submarines were alarmingly active. The new arrival was Cecil Gray, a close friend of Philip Heseltine's. This friendship with Heseltine didn't discourage Lawrence from making himself useful to the future composer, music critic and biographer who, at twenty-three, was ten years younger than Lawrence. Gray had chosen Cornwall as a place to escape the London war fever and to pursue his creative work in more peaceful surroundings. He had a defective heart and had been declared exempt from military service. While Gray was in London seeing his mother and attending to final details involving the move, Lawrence got William Henry to check on Gray's luggage in Penzance. Lawrence promised to see the goods safely to Bosigran. Then he went to Benny's in St. Ives and eyed several tables, beds and mattresses. Should he buy them for Gray? He needed to know by return mail.

In his autobiography, *Musical Chairs*, Cecil Gray wrote that Lawrence "particularly endeared himself to me through the extraordinary kindness and helpfulness he showed me in dealing with the practical problems of life." Lawrence couldn't do enough for Gray. Not only did he buy the furnishings, but he decided on the paint for the upstairs, and he made sketches and recommendations for settling the house comfortably. Lawrence even scrubbed the floors. Gray was only too delighted to leave these matters in such capable hands. "In retrospect, however," Gray observed, "I am inclined to suspect that in addition to his genuine fondness for such occupations there was also a certain streak of mystical self-abasement involved."[3]

Mrs. Tarry, their former landlady in Hampstead, more Frieda's friend than Lawrence's, came to visit during the first week of June. It was a week too long for him, but he declared himself "philosophic to the minor evils."[4] Lawrence had received papers for another medical examination. He immediately got Dr. John Dyer Rice, the St. Ives doctor, to send an unfit notice to the military in Penzance. There was nothing he could do now but wait developments. It left him with an uneasy feeling as he worked on his tiny book of philosophy, part mysticism and part metaphysics, a book which may have been burned in the chimney at Higher Tregerthen as the manuscript didn't survive.

He didn't have long to wait. The military refused to accept Dr. Rice's certificate of unfitness, and Lawrence was directed to report for a medical examination on June 23 as previously notified. Another Bodmin experience was more than he wanted to face. He would see a specialist in London and get an unfit certificate issued from there. Lawrence immediately wrote his London friends of his impending visit, including Middleton Murry. He would be staying with Dollie Radford, and would Murry ring him up there so they could meet?

Lawrence and Frieda went to Benny's in St. Ives on the morning of June 14. There they bought a variety of furnishings for Gray and arranged to have them transported to Bosigran Castle. He had spent more than ten pounds, but he hoped Gray wouldn't be disappointed with the purchases. "I shall be glad if you can come down again immediately," he wrote Gray, "and we can install you." Lawrence's opinion of Heseltine was undergoing a change. "Let me know how it is: also tell me about Heseltine. I am feeling kindly about him again."[5]

Lawrence stayed with Dollie Radford while in London, and she packed a lunch for his long train ride back to Cornwall. Frieda had remained at Tregerthen—they were again pressed for money. "Although I don't think I got much good out of the doctors," he wrote Radford upon his return, "still something in the visit made me happier, a new, freer, happier feeling between us, growing like leaves."[6] Bodmin no longer troubled him deeply. He was convinced that all would be well.

Lawrence waved good-bye to Frieda on June 23, followed the footpath to Zennor, and rode to Penzance with Tom Berryman. This time his ordeal was brief. Lawrence waited only two hours at Bodmin Barracks for the doctors to ask their questions and to make their humiliating probes. He was declared unfit for duty, but the day of an outright rejection had passed. He was now classified as 3C—able to perform some light non-military service. This new classification didn't trouble Lawrence. So many men were waiting to serve in this catagory, and it was doubtful if he would ever be called. He got back to the cottage by nightfall, and again he and Frieda were jubilant.

Lawrence wrote J. B. Pinker on the 28th of June. He had come to the end of the road financially; he needed money again, and the outlook was no brighter than ever. Would Pinker give him an advance? Then Lawrence asked if there was any news of his *Look! We Have Come Through!* "I have been having some bother about medical re-examination," he told Pinker, "but have got rejected again. I wouldn't do anything for the army, any way." He felt the world was changing, and there was room for optimism. Ezra Pound had asked to publish his story "Once." Should he let him? "How and where he will bring it out I don't know, his letter is so foolish—as usual."[7]

Edward Marsh sent Lawrence a check for seven pounds and fifteen shillings for poems in *Georgian Poetry.* He already owed Marsh money, but the anthologist insisted that Lawrence take the royalties. This windfall wouldn't carry him for long, and in a letter to Kotelian- sky on July 3, he expressed doubts about his agent. "I wrote and told Pinker I must have more money. He does not answer. Probably he does not want to advance any more. . . . My relations with that little parvenu snob of a procureur of books were always strained, best have them broken."[8]

Like Orioli, Pinker found his dealings with Lawrence trouble- some. There was a lack of trust between the two and with good reasons for both parties. Pinker wasn't always efficient and he sometimes misled his client—deliberately, Lawrence felt, when his American publisher Benjamin W. Huebsch and Pinker were negotiat- ing *Women in Love.* But Lawrence enjoyed getting the better of Pinker whenever he could. When Lawrence tried to interest Austin Harrison of the *English Review* in his "The Reality of Peace" articles, he wrote Harrison without Pinker's knowledge, and later the agent was in- formed by Harrison that financial arrangements were between Law- rence and the *English Review.* Relations were further strained when Lawrence circumvented Pinker by negotiating directly with Huebsch for the publication of *New Poems,* and with Harrison for two essays on American literature. The break between Lawrence and Pinker didn't occur until January 1920, but by that time both men had had enough.

Cecil Gray came down from London, and Lawrence happily saw him installed at Bosigran. "Our friendship ripened quickly," Gray noted in *Musical Chairs,* "and within a very short time we used to meet virtually every day, either at his place or at mine, over a period of many months."[9] A friendship did ripen, but during those four and a half months in Cornwall from early July to mid-October, when both men were neighbors, Lawrence often had other priorities. Boris de Croustchoff, Russian bibliographer, whom Lawrence knew through Heseltine, was a houseguest at Bosigran and Gray wanted Lawrence to visit. But the days were sunny and William Henry needed him in the fields. "I feel pledged to help with the hay while the weather lasts," Lawrence wrote Gray on July 11, "so will postpone coming to Bosigran for a day or two. You and Krustchoff come over here—come to tea and supper any day: and we will come out to you on Sunday, if that is all right for you."[10]

The friendship between Gray and Lawrence didn't survive for long—there were too many complications—and it never reached the intensity of a Middleton Murry or William Henry relationship. As early as the spring of 1918, the union was all but over. Lawrence later asked Gray to run errands for him, such as packing the belongings left at Higher Tregerthen, but Lawrence couldn't conceal his irritation. On March 12, 1918, he wrote Gray: "I don't know why you and I don't get on very well when we are together. But it seems we don't. It seems we are best apart."[11] Gray felt that Lawrence expected his friends to give up their personalities if friendship was to survive. To surrender completely. But Catherine Carswell named Gray as one of those who failed Lawrence. Carswell felt that Gray didn't give him "the responsive friendship that he craved and deserved."[12] Gray claimed that he assisted Lawrence during the difficult time when the military authorities expelled her hero from Cornwall and the only thanks he got in return was "to be pilloried and caricatured" in two of Lawrence's books. "Apart from the chapter alluded to in *Kangaroo*, ("The Nightmare") which is more or less accurate *reportage* and merely represents me as a faintly unpleasant nonentity (James Sharpe), I am portrayed in *Aaron's Rod* under the guise of a musician called Cyril Scott." Gray believed if the composer who did bear that name had brought a libel action against Lawrence, the real Cyril Scott would have been "awarded substantial damages, for a more nauseating specimen of the human race could hardly be imagined."[13]

Gray did make himself useful at the time of the expulsion by giving the Lawrences money and writing his mother to arrange for them to stay in her vacant London flat at Earl's Court. But he soon felt that he was being used by Lawrence and that too much was expected of him. More than he realized. Shortly after Lawrence's arrival in London, in a letter to Catherine Carswell, another Rananim crew was named. They would all settle on a slope in the Andes. "Gray can find £1000."[14] Gray was astonished to learn that he had been appointed to finance the expedition. His parents had money, but the young composer's allowance was only two hundred pounds a year. He now had little interest in Rananim, though he had agreed to such an adventure earlier. The thought of spending the rest of his life in the Andes with Lawrence, Frieda, William Henry, the Carswells, Koteliansky, and others wasn't Gray's idea of paradise.

Hilda Doolittle, the American poet H. D., then married to English author Richard Aldington, had met Lawrence in the summer of 1914. She was fascinated by Lawrence and would have become romantically involved with him if he had asked her. But he always wanted cerebral relationships with the women who admired him. H. D. lent the Lawrences a room in her flat at 44 Mecklenburgh Square upon their arrival in London. She, tiring of Aldington and realizing that her love for Lawrence would never be returned, attached herself to Gray, much to Lawrence's displeasure. Gray fell in love with her and asked her to live with him at Bosigran. H. D. went to Cornwall with Gray in 1918 and began to write what would eventually be published as *Bid Me to Live*, in 1960. Barbara Guest described the work in her H. D. biography *Herself Defined*: "The book in its last phase is a hymn to Lawrence, who would not be her lover, but whose genius she would worship."[15]

An argument erupted between Lawrence and Gray at Mecklenburgh Square. Gray was critical of Lawrence's *Look! We Have Come Through!* "I don't care what you accept or don't accept, either: it bores me a bit. But don't go throwing about accusations and calling me a liar gratuitously," Lawrence wrote on November 6. "Perhaps you are right to resent the impertinence of the 'Look!' None the less, we have come through."[16] Gray had been careful not to rile Lawrence in Cornwall— in fact, Gray had made himself completely agreeable. Now the young composer was resisting his friend, openly defying Lawrence by falling in love with H. D. and threatening to steal her from the flock. Perhaps Gray also wanted to extricate himself before Lawrence found out about him and Frieda.

Paul Delany, in his *D. H. Lawrence's Nightmare: The Writer and his Circle in the Years of the Great War*, surveyed the likelihood that Frieda and Gray had a brief affair. Frieda was left alone all too often during that long summer of 1917 and she frequently went to Bosigran to spend afternoons with Gray while Lawrence was in the hayfields with William Henry. She was at Bosigran the day the cottage was ransacked by the authorities; the day Lawrence went to Penzance with William Henry and Mabel Hocking—a detail that both Stanley and Mary Hocking remembered. In "The Nightmare" chapter of *Kangaroo*,

Lawrence also places Frieda at Bosigran at the time of the raid: "It was evident, Harriet (Frieda) had had a bad shock. She had walked in the afternoon across to Sharpe's (Gray's) place, three miles away: and had got back just at nightfall, expecting Somers home by seven."[17]

Gray, who claimed to be tired of Lawrence's "dark gods," and "sensuous underworlds," wrote Lawrence accusing him "of allowing himself to become the object of a kind of esoteric female cult, an Adonis, Atthis, Dionysos religion of which he was the central figure, a Jesus Christ to a regiment of Mary Magdalenes."[18] Gray had in mind Esther Andrews, Catherine Carswell, Lady Cynthia Asquith, and most of all Hilda Doolittle. Lawrence quickly responded with a testy letter explaining his following. "As for me and my 'women,' I know what they are and aren't, and though there is a certain messiness, there is a further reality." Perhaps Lawrence already knew about Gray and Frieda—he had looked the other way on previous occasions when Frieda had embarked on sexual adventures. "And both you and Frieda need to go one world deeper in knowledge." Wife and quarrelsome friend had more to learn: they both inhabited "an underworld which is forever an underworld, never to be made open and whole."[19]

In 1915, H. D. was becoming emotionally preoccupied with Lawrence—at the time her marriage was deteriorating. Before marrying Aldington, she had wanted to marry Ezra Pound but the romance failed. Janice S. Robertson, in her biography *H. D. The Life and Work of an American Poet*, weaves a close relationship between Lawrence and H. D. by relying mostly on their poetry and prose—the two were exchanging manuscripts for several years. There is nothing to suggest that Lawrence and H. D. were ever intimate. H. D. did form a romantic picture of Lawrence at Tregerthen: she saw him as a man of vision writing without comfort in his cottage while the fierce winds swept across the dark Cornish moors and over the empty mine shafts. It was during the Lawrences' stay at Mecklenburgh Square that Frieda shattered H. D.'s vision. She told H. D. that Lawrence cared only for men. There were now two distinct personalities in H. D.'s thoughts: the Lawrence as a man alone, and the Lawrence with a wife. They never saw H. D. again after she went to Cornwall with Cecil Gray and became pregnant with Gray's child. Although she continued to write about Lawrence in her poems and stories, H. D. did her best to keep her feelings hidden from her homosexual companion, Bryher Ellerman. Bryher was puzzled when she met Lawrence for the first time, in

1926, and he requested that she make quite sure to send Hilda his love.

Esther Andrews, now in Paris, had been commissioned to ask Lawrence for some stories for *Seven Arts,* and the stories were to be sent either to Paris or to Waldo Frank in New York. Lawrence instructed Pinker to send manuscripts to Frank at once. In a letter to Frank, on July 27, Lawrence discussed his suppressed novel, *The Rainbow*: "I don't think the war altered it, from its pre-war statement." He knew he was writing "a destructive work" at the time, therefore the title *The Rainbow*—"in reference to the Flood." He told Frank that he wanted to come to America and that he didn't "believe in Uncle Samdom, of course. But if the rainbow hangs in the heavens, it hangs over the western continent."[20]

Chatto and Windus wrote J. B. Pinker that they would publish *Look! We Have Come Through!* if two of the poems, "Song of a Man Who is Loved" and "Meeting among the Mountains," were omitted. They also requested the omission or modification of several other lines "referring to purely physical phenomena" that the public might find "objectionable."[21] If the author would agree to these changes, the collection would be set for the autumn list. Pinker forwarded the letter to Lawrence. There was one poem that Lawrence felt should be included, the poem "Song of a Man Who is Loved." Would Pinker try to convince the firm to leave it in the book? And if they persisted, get them to say what they objected to in the poem. But even as he wrote his agent, Lawrence knew that it would be foolhardy to resist too strongly with any publisher after *The Rainbow.*

Lawrence had completed his manuscript of philosophy called "At the Gates." It would be a book of about 140 pages and he was anxious to see it in print. "I don't suppose publishers are dying to publish such a book," he wrote Pinker, "but it just *might* be well received."[22] And on the same day, August 27, Lawrence reported to Catherine Carswell that Frieda was recovering from neuritis in her leg. "Did I tell you we've got a piano—old, red silk front—five guineas—nice old musty twang with it."[23] Then two days later, in a letter to Dollie Radford, Lawrence had bits of local news. It had been raining hard, the corn at the farm had been cut but not taken in, and his garden had been smashed by the rain. They had had few visitors, only Gray and "Meredith Starr, and his wife Lady Mary, the Earl of Stamford's daughter, and a half-caste, half negro. I don't like them very much."[24]

Meredith Starr hadn't yet transformed himself into the author of several books, including *The Future of the Novel*—a book in which he had nothing to say concerning the work of his nearby neighbor. "They fast," Lawrence wrote Lady Cynthia Asquith, "or eat nettles: they descend naked into old mine-shafts, and there meditate for hours and hours, upon their own transcendent infinitude." The Starrs would "descend" upon the Lawrences, "like a swarm of locusts" and "devour all the food on the shelf or board: they even gave a concert and made the most dreadful fools of themselves in St. Ives: violent correspondence in the *St. Ives Times*."[25]

When asked if he remembered Starr and Lady Mary, Stanley Hocking declared: "I should think I do! I remember those two! They were living in a little cottage at Treveal—about a mile east of us. One night in St. Ives, while the old Pavilion was still in existence at Porthminister Beach, those two put on a concert. Lawrence, Frieda, William Henry, myself, and I believe my two sisters, Mabel and Mary, drove to see it in our usual horse and rally cart. And of all the damned nonsense and rubbish in the world it proved to be. It was ridiculous! The two were hooted out before the concert was over. It was certainly an amusing episode, and it got described in the local press. They did the most senseless songs and dances you ever saw. They brought in a rather well-known violinist here in town, and he played some violin solos which were very highly respected. But apart from the violin solos, the whole concert was rubbish. Starr and Lady Mary tried to put on the whole concert themselves. Lawrence was very disgusted with it. 'Had I known,' he said, 'I would have never gone to see it.' "

P. O. Eddy also recalled Starr and Lady Mary. "The couple down at Treveal weren't Zennor people either. As youngsters, some of us would go down there and talk with them. I remember we went down one night, and we saw that they had big stones on their roof. Starr had covered his roof with a tarpaulin to keep the rain out and had used stones to keep the tarpaulin from blowing away. He said he had put little stones on first, and the tarpaulin had stayed down for six weeks. 'Now I have larger stones on the roof,' he said. He didn't think of mending the roof! Things like this amused we Cornish people."

"The summer has gone quickly," Lawrence wrote Koteliansky on September 23. Frieda was better and he was well. "We have had nobody to see us since Esther Andrews was here in the spring: that is, nobody to stay." Gray visited frequently, and of course, the "rather dreadful" Starrs. Murry and Katherine Mansfield had written "once or twice" and then no more. "The past is past. So little of it has survived into the present.—I am fond of the people at the farm." He was correcting proofs for *Look! We Have Come Through!* "I have worked like a labourer through corn and hay harvest: corn yet remains to be carried in."[26] The Gertlers and Ottolines were out of his life. The world no longer existed for him.


## XI


It was the spirit of the war that tortured Lawrence, not the long lists of casualties that were reported daily from the front. The mass hypnosis that drove men to slaughter shocked him more than the tragic waste of lives. He cursed the mindlessness and somnambulism of his countrymen and insisted that none of the millions who took part in the struggle really experienced it. He saw the conflict as a suicide pact among nations and the end of the old world. He was convinced that one war must always breed another and that there was little likelihood of lasting peace. It was the end of democracy, liberty, and freedom. The world would never be the same for him again. There would be no recovery; no returning to the England he knew and loved. "The war is just hell for me." Lawrence admitted this to Edward Marsh when the conflict was only three weeks old. "I don't see why I should be so disturbed—but I am. I can't get away from it for a minute: live in a sort of coma, like one of those nightmares when you can't move. I hate it—everything."[1]

Lawrence became more troubled as the cries of patriotism grew louder and the carnage increased. Except for the six-week period when *The Rainbow* was at issue before the public and in court, most of his letters carry some mention of the war. At times, he sounded hysterical as he lashed out at the stupidity of the giant powers and the mentality of statesmen. But he was determined not to humiliate himself by serving his country. Better to be killed than to become part of the mob. Even a simple medical examination was enough to drive him into a frenzy. This was an invasion of his privacy, another humiliation, and as he sometimes proclaimed when things were not to his liking: "I won't have it!"

But submit he did. Three times he faced the doctors and escaped. The picture of Lawrence, helmeted, with rifle in hand, and going over the top for his country, against Frieda's fatherland, would have been difficult to bring into focus for those who received his letters. His anger increased as disaster followed disaster. In a letter to Lady Ottoline Morrell, a week after the *Lusitania* was torpedoed by a German submarine with the loss of 1,198 lives, Lawrence declared: "And we don't want to be worked up into this fury, this destructive madness of rage. Yet we must, we are goaded on and on. I am mad with rage myself. I would like to kill a million Germans—two million."[2] It was an extravagant statement for a man with a German wife. Perhaps Lady Ottoline smiled when she read the letter and thought of Frieda.

It was a bitter time for Lawrence, and he often had reason to feel discouraged. He had no money, *The Rainbow* had been banned, his health was bad, he was having trouble getting his work published, and his struggle with sexual preference was causing his marriage to be shaky. Yet he did bear all these things with courage. He was aware that he often reacted unreasonably and irrationally, but there was never any lying to himself. He responded to the war as he felt it, even if it cost him a friendship, as it did with Edward Marsh who fully endorsed the government policies while working as a civil servant. "For me," Lawrence wrote Lady Cynthia Asquith, "it is better to die than to do something which is utterly a violation to my soul." Death wasn't a violation for him. "On the other hand, war cannot be thought of, for me, without the utmost repulsion and desecration of one's being. For me, the war is wrong, and nothing, neither life nor death, can make it right."[3]

Frieda shared Lawrence's horror of the war, and her German background placed her in a difficult position. Though she had lived in Nottingham for a number of years with her first English husband, and now in a wartime England with her second, her loyalties to her native land were strong. Frieda disliked the Kaiser, but she was proud that her younger sister, Johanna, had married Max Schreibershofen, aide-de-camp to the crown prince. Two von Richthofen cousins had joined the German Air Force, and both became leaders. One of these cousins was Manfred von Richthofen, the most famous of all German flyers during World War I, the Red Baron.

"I used to think war so glorious," Frieda wrote Edward Marsh on September 13, 1914, "my father such a hero with his iron cross and his hand that a bullet had torn." But the glory was gone for her now, and she hated the waste of lives. She told Marsh that he must not hate her native land. "We are frightfully nice people, but it is so difficult for the English to understand anything that is *not* English."[4]

But this was written at the beginning of the war before a generation of young men had been killed on the battlefields and hatred for everything German had solidified at home. Frieda, with her tactlessness, taxed the patience of several of Lawrence's friends. Violet Hunt, a reader for Ford Madox Hueffer's (later Ford Madox Ford) *English Review,* had known Lawrence when he was teaching in Croydon. Violet Hunt, in the company of Hueffer and Mrs. H. G. Wells, visited Greatham one day when Lawrence was away. During a conversation with Frieda, Hunt mentioned Hueffer's popular poem "Antwerp," a poem inspired by the sight of Belgian refugees at Charing Cross Station. "Dirty Belgians!" Frieda was reported to have said. "Who cares for them!"[5] Hueffer claimed he went to an outhouse to escape Frieda's tirade of pro-Germanism because he was wearing the uniform of his country. Frieda, in a 1955 letter to Harry T. Moore, insisted there was no outhouse at Greatham, that the visit occurred before Hueffer joined the forces, and denied ever having made such a remark about Belgians.

Frieda was often indiscreet in parading her Teutonic background before acquaintances and strangers. She would sing German songs, dress in her Bavarian costume, and proudly reveal her family's baronial connections. She was too outgoing to keep her divided sympathies to herself; too naive to realize that she was often the enemy in the eyes of those who were in her company. David Garnett, in his book *Flowers of the Forest,* wrote that from the beginning of the war Frieda "found herself already being cold-shouldered and disliked because of her German origin." The Lawrences visited Garnett and one of his Imperial College friends at Garnett's flat and when they left the friend called down to Frieda " 'Auf Wiedersehen Gnädige Baronin!' and Frieda called back gaily to us in German."[6] The remark prompted the visits of several detectives who were suspicious of Garnett and his visitors. It was obviously not the time or place for German farewells.

Emile Delavenay, when assessing Lawrence's response to the times, pointed out that "Lawrence never openly, publicly or at any real risk to himself, spoke or wrote about the war: there is simply no evidence of courage in his reactions to the war."[7] Aside from bitterly complaining about the war in letters to friends, and adopting the idea of founding a colony, a Rananim, to escape England, Lawrence took no active part. He seemed paralyzed by the times. The nearest he came to responding was with Bertrand Russell.

Lawrence met Russell through Lady Ottoline in 1916. The two men shared similar views on the war, and soon the idea of forming a series of lectures in London appealed to them both. Russell would lecture on Ethics and Lawrence on Immortality. But Russell's brand of pacifism, and philosophical differences between the miner's son and the heir to an earldom, sparked controversy. An emotional upheaval awaited Lawrence when he went to Cambridge to see Russell and his friends. It was there that he met the noted economist John Maynard Keynes. Lawrence "was morose from the outset and said very little," Keynes recalled, "apart from indefinite expressions of irritable dissent, all the morning." Both Keynes and Russell tried to draw him into conversation, but he sat on a sofa "in rather a crouching position with his head down" loathing Keynes.[8] The economist felt that Lawrence was jealous because both Keynes and Russell were friends of Lady Ottoline and part of the Bloomsbury-Cambridge circle of intellectuals, which Lawrence was not, and because Lawrence disliked Cambridge for its hold on David Garnett. Keynes' homosexuality filled Lawrence with loathing and Garnett's friendship with Francis Birrell worried him. "It is foolish of you to say that it doesn't matter either way—the men loving men," Lawrence wrote Garnett on April 19, 1915. "It doesn't matter in the public way. But it matters so much, David, to the man himself—at any rate to us northern nations— that it is like a blow of triumphant decay, when I meet Birrell or the others." Garnett must escape these people and become whole by loving a woman. "Truly I didn't know it was wrong, till I saw K. (Keynes) that morning in Cambridge. It was one of the crises in my life."[9]

Lawrence continued writing to Russell on the need for social justice and revolution, but the hope that the two would join forces soon faded. One letter to Russell, written in Padstow, Cornwall, revealed Lawrence's ability to lash out. Russell had written that he contemplated suicide, and only pride and obstinacy prevented him. "I didn't like your letter," Lawrence began. "What's the good of living as you do, any way. I don't believe your lectures *are* good. They are nearly over, aren't they?" He advised Russell to become "an outlaw" and "not a teacher or preacher." It was now time for the new. The old self must be left behind. "Do stop working and writing altogether and become a creature instead of a mechanical instrument." Then Lawrence asked Russell to remember him. "Oh, and I want to ask you, when you make out your will, do leave me enough to live on. I want you to live for ever. But I want you to make me in some part your heir."[10]

Recalling his association with Lawrence, Bertrand Russell wrote in *Portraits from Memory and Other Essays*: "There were in Lawrence at that time two attitudes to the war: on the one hand, he could not be whole-heartedly patriotic, because his wife was German; but on the other hand, he had such a hatred of mankind that he tended to think both sides must be right in so far as they hated each other." Then Russell opened a hornet's nest: "The world between the wars was attracted to madness. Of this attraction Nazism was the most emphatic expression. Lawrence was a suitable exponent of this cult of insanity."[11]

Lawrence's defenders were quick to refute Russell's charge and to call it absurd. But there were too many examples in Lawrence's work and letters to quiet the uproar. His Mexican novel, *The Plumed Serpent*, led some of his readers to think of Lawrence as a fascist. The torchlight parades, the screaming crowds and waving banners in the book were suggestive of Hitler's rallies. Attila and Bismarck are given praise in his *Movements in European History*, and a strong man to save Europe is mentioned at the end of *Aaron's Rod*. His letters to Rolf Gardiner, a pioneer of Land Service Camps for Youth in Northern Europe following World War I, and several anti-Semitic remarks Lawrence let slip in letters to friends have been cited to substantiate Russell's opinion. "As for calling Lawrence an exponent of Nazism," Frieda Lawrence wrote in an article published in *Harper's Magazine*, in 1953, "that is pure nonsense —you might as well call St. Augustine a Nazi."[12] But Frieda herself saw Hitler as a misunderstood genius in 1936, and she expressed admiration for *Mein Kampf*, finding the book "effective in its ideology."[13]

"It was in 1915 the old world ended," Lawrence wrote in "The Nightmare" chapter of *Kangaroo*. "In the winter of 1915-1916 the spirit of the old London collapsed; the city, in some way, perished, perished from being a heart of the world, and became a vortex of broken passions, lusts, hopes, fears, and horrors."[14] He and Frieda were planning to go to America, to Florida, but when the opportunity came he couldn't break away. "We are not going to Florida immediately,"

Lawrence wrote Lady Cynthia Asquith in December 1915. They were going to Cornwall. "There are several others—young men and women—who are anxious to come with us, and we shall have to wait for them: just a month or two." The war had convinced Lawrence that there was need of a new life elsewhere, away from London, and he was going to live that life in a new spirit. "We go down there next week. Some members of our Florida expedition are coming down too—we begin the new life in Cornwall. It is real."[15]

## XII

"Lawrence and Frieda didn't look like the ordinary people of West Cornwall," said Stanley Hocking. "They were different. There was nobody in the locality who dressed the way he did. His corduroy suit and slouch hat and beard and Victorian collar and tie were unusual. His collar and tie reminded me of old Gladstone. Then there were the submarines sinking our ships right in view of Lawrence's cottage. People knew he was English enough, but of course since he was married to a German they didn't know if his loyalties had remained English. And then the remark was being passed: 'You never know what people are up to. They could have a secret code for signaling to the German submarines and giving the position of our ships.' "

"Lawrence didn't mix with every class of people," said P. O. Eddy. "You couldn't classify him as one of us. He was peculiar. Very reserved. I don't think he mixed with many people other than the Hockings. He would come and go with the Berrymans for his shop needs. But he didn't contact more people than he had to contact. The Lawrences weren't Zennor people."

"Local people in Zennor knew that Frieda was a German," declared Ivor Short, "and they immediately called her a German spy. The trouble is in a small place people do nothing but gossip and gossip. They said the only reason why the Lawrences lived there was because their cottage overlooked the Atlantic. The gossip went so far that some people said there was nothing but signaling going on all the time while they were there. People around here didn't like the

Germans. After all, we were fighting Germany then. Frieda was a German. But the Lawrences never said anything against the people here, and they didn't like the war."

"It's only natural for one neighbor to be curious in knowing what the next neighbor is doing," said Arthur Eddy. "There was talk. Naturally, the people talked. You can depend on that. And William Henry was told to keep quiet about Lawrence being watched. The police told him that he could be locked up too. They were suspicious of Lawrence, and William Henry was going around with him. The authorities were watching them both. I don't think they expected William Henry would do any harm, but he was with the man."

"There were a lot of ships being sunk off the coast," recalled Ivor Short. "That's where the Lawrences got into trouble. The ships were going down like tenpins all the time. That section of the coast was a hunting ground for the submarines. When the ships were going up channel it was the best time for the Germans to operate. Every time a ship would go down, Lawrence would wince."

"There weren't many strangers in Zennor," stated P. O. Eddy. "But the only thing we heard was that the authorities had been down and told poor old Lawrence to leave. When the submarines started torpedoing the boats was when the fear of war began. I heard people say they used to see a little lamp flashing at the Lawrences."

Cecil Gray's appearance in Zennor aroused local suspicion, particularly since Gray was very friendly with the bearded man who had a German wife, and with the other strange young man, Heseltine, who had come to live nearby. It was a small community living in constant fear of an invasion, and the slightest departure from the routine of daily activity was looked upon with suspicion. When Gray installed window curtains of different colors, it was regarded by some people as a way of signaling to the submarines. Why weren't these three young men at the front? Why weren't they engaged in some form of useful employment to help their country? There were people in Zennor who shook their heads and wondered. "West Cornwall decided that it was being delivered straight into German hands," Lawrence wrote in *Kangaroo*. "Not that West Cornwall would really have minded that so terribly. No; it wasn't that it feared the Germans. It was that it hated the sight of these recalcitrant young men."[1]

Several people in Zennor who lived through this difficult time and who had read "The Nightmare" chapter of *Kangaroo* resented Lawrence's opinion of the Cornish reaction to the war. "We weren't as bad as Lawrence said," replied an elderly customer over his pint at the Tinners Arms.

Giuseppe Orioli thought otherwise. Orioli wrote in his autobiography, *Adventures of a Bookseller*, 1937, that he remembered "a nice old woman at Zennor" who stated she would like to hang the Kaiser and eat his heart—a woman who had lost no relatives in the war. Orioli also claimed that he knew a lecturer on Italian art who had given up his native German citizenship to become an English subject and who had settled in Cornwall. But the Cornish suspected him of spying and he was watched and his cottage searched on several occasions. ("I never heard of such a thing!" declared Stanley Hocking.) The lecturer's heart was weak and he was unable to walk to nearby Penzance. When the Penzance merchants refused to deliver his groceries, two sympathetic girls brought his food to him. One day the police found a note he had written for the girls, and the authorities decided that the word *macaroons* was a code word for the gasoline which he was suspected of supplying to German submarines. "From that day onward he was tortured" by the police and his neighbors "into such a state of depression and misery that he killed himself."[2]

German submarines became more active along the Bristol Channel between Land's End and St. Ives, and suspicion increased with every ship that went down. "We're all going to be butchered," a farmer told William Henry on market day in Penzance. "Trust no one," he warned Hocking. And in St. Ives a fisherman told the Shorts that he had seen a small boat offshore near Tregerthen one night, and a man had left the boat and swum ashore. "The Germans are getting ready to invade us," he said. "They have their spies out."

"A lot of people," said Stanley Hocking, "started thinking that the Germans would invade us quietly and secretly by submarines on our Cornish beaches. Probably send little raiding bands ashore, just to knock the wind out of us and to terrify us. Then people began thinking: what's to stop those fellows on a quiet night from running ashore in one of our nice little coves? They could come up to the farms and cut our throats. It was possible."

Members of the Hocking and Eddy families were amused when hearing of the many reasons Zennor people suspected the Lawrences of being actively engaged as spies. The Cornish found "The Nightmare" chapter of *Kangaroo* highly exaggerated and more a work of fiction than accurate reporting. Heseltine and Gray agreed with Lawrence's impressions, but both men had little reason to share local concerns. Heseltine was in Cornwall only a short time when worries of an invasion were on the minds of those living on the farms and in Zennor village, and Gray had little use for the local peasantry. He felt that Lawrence was "foolishly lax" in his dealings with the farm family and William Henry.[3] "Now the tales began to go round full-tilt against Somers," Lawrence wrote in *Kangaroo*. "A chimney of his house was tarred to keep out the damp: that was a signal to the Germans. He and his wife carried food to supply German submarines. They had secret stores of petrol in the cliff."[4]

When hearing of this, Stanley Hocking was surprised. "My God, this is getting a bit thick! But I can guess how such a silly remark came into being. If it happened, which I very much doubt. During those war years, with so many ships being torpedoed, all sorts of articles were being washed ashore. Bales of hay, cases of matches, and slabs of candle grease. I can truthfully say I came across these myself. They weren't worth much. And yes, some tins of petrol were being washed ashore. This was in 1917. The petrol had probably been in a steamer that was sunk on its way to France. The tins had been smashed about and were leaking. You could smell petrol when you went down by the cliff on certain days."

"Don't you believe it," said Ivor Short. "It was the people on those farms who suspected the Lawrences. The people would gossip, and they suspected any stranger. Anyone who would come in their midst." When questioned closely about this, Hocking gave ground. "Perhaps some people did criticize us for being friendly, but we had no reason to suspect the Lawrences. They were perfectly nice to us."

When asked what he thought of Lawrence's statement in *Kangaroo* that "each farm was bitter jealous of each other," Stanley Hocking answered with irritation.[5] "I think Lawrence was jumping to conclusions. We were all friends and neighbors on the farms in those days. I don't think our neighbors were interested at all in how friendly we were with the Lawrences. Not those in the vicinity of Tregerthen. After all, Lawrence's cottage was only one little item in the country-side. People didn't visit much because everybody had so much work to do during the war years. We had to plow and to plant about three times the ordinary acreage. I think Lawrence invented this. People in Zennor village did gossip, and Lawrence was very sensitive. He might have imagined that the entire parish was against him. But the few farmers and farmers' wives and families close by didn't see Lawrence enough to suspect or hate him. People didn't move around much in those days. Many farmers would never have the occasion to see the Lawrences at all—not the ordinary people. Mind you, when Lawrence and Frieda would go into town, to say the least, they looked a bit outlandish. Nine times out of ten, Frieda would be wearing her bright-red stockings into St. Ives. And some would ask: 'Well! Who are they!' Then the inevitable question: 'Are they married?' I think some people worried more about this than the spy business."

In *Musical Chairs*, Cecil Gray admitted that "there was just a shred of justification for the distrust and suspicion which Lawrence had aroused in official circles, apart from his German wife, his reputation as a writer of immoral tendencies, and the unfortunate episode in which we had been involved together"—Gray meant the showing of a light at Bosigran when the Lawrences were visiting. The young musician felt that Lawrence was "indiscreet in speech when in the company of people whom he may sometimes wrongly have supposed to be trustworthy." More than once Lawrence revealed to Gray plans of "initiating a disruptive, pacifist and nihilist campaign in the industrial North, with a view to bringing about a speedy end to the War." Gray claimed that Lawrence was determined to embark upon such an adventure and when asked if he would accompany Lawrence, Gray "agreed unhesitatingly" to the plan, for "such was the extent of his influence over me in these days."[6]

"Lawrence didn't hold his tongue altogether," said Stanley Hocking. "But I don't think he made any remarks so people would suspect him. He would talk openly with William Henry and my dear old Uncle Henry—Mother's brother. But he didn't converse with other people. I do know that Lawrence was very upset when Lloyd George was brought into the government and Asquith was out. I remember that. Lawrence said: 'This is the end of my England as I know it.' He didn't like Lloyd George. Why, I don't know. He referred to Lloyd George as 'a dirty little Welsh rat.' He said the man wasn't fit for office. And when we had our little Christmas party in the tower, before we finished, the conversation touched upon a variety of subjects. Some of which—shall I say—had an international touch? The Americans, Robert Mountsier and Esther Andrews, thought their country should join in the war against Germany. This made it very uncomfortable and difficult for Frieda. I remember Lawrence saying: 'All wars are futile and useless. They are never caused by the ordinary people. They never want wars. Wars are caused by blundering statesmen.' Then Lawrence said to Mountsier: 'What will you have? More destruction?' "

Cecil Gray believed that some of Lawrence's long talks were overheard by the authorities. "One of the less engaging aspects of the Cornish character consists in a mania for spying and listening at keyholes or windows." Gray was certain that both he and Lawrence were under surveillance. Nothing ever came of Lawrence's plan of disrupting the industrial apparatus of England—"it was all talk," wrote Gray, "mere hot air," but some of Lawrence's "wilder discourse" could have been relayed to military headquarters. Cecil Gray felt that the times "only required a leader with a sense of direction to render" such disruptive plans and Lawrence was "potentially such a leader." Then Gray suggested: "He was, indeed, the stuff of which Hitlers are made, especially at that time when his great gifts were unrecognized and he was on the verge of penury."[7]

"The Germans were winning in late 1916," said Stanley Hocking. "There was no radio then, but we could see from our daily newspapers that the front was shifting. And there were the horrible lists of casualties in the newspapers. It was terrifying. Thousands of young men listed as killed or wounded. Some of them were young men we knew. Things got to be very difficult in 1917. All of 1917 was quite bad. In early 1916, up there in the country, we scarcely knew there was a war going on. We were far away from it all. We became scared in late 1916. I don't remember much submarine activity in the early part of 1916. What aroused suspicion was that Lawrence moved into Higher Tregerthen, and gradually the submarines began sinking our ships. There was a genuine fear of being invaded or perhaps being shelled out of existence. We were told that the Germans had millions of everything, and they could easily put more men into the field. To offset this opinion, I heard the old men talking: 'No boy, they'll never land in this country. They'll never get this country. What do you think our navy would be doing if they tried to land here?' These were the general comforting statements that were being made."

Then Stanley Hocking paused for a moment and smiled. "Shall I tell you an amusing story that goes against the Americans a bit?" When told to go ahead, he said: "In those days we had several American submarine chasers based at Penzance, and quite a lot of the Americans came ashore for a pint at the local hotel. This was towards the end of 1917. The beer was duly poured by a rather attractive barmaid. One of the Americans took a sip and said: 'Say, Miss, this goddamn beer tastes flat!' And the barmaid replied: 'No wonder, my boy. It's been over here three years waiting for you to come!' The

general feeling was that America should have entered the war long before it did. If Germany had beaten England, America would have been
in trouble."

Cecil Gray claimed to have learned after the war that he,
Lawrence and Frieda were believed to be the heads of a spy ring, and
that Gray was in danger of losing his life. One evening "an expedition
of local worthies, armed with scythes and pitchforks" decided to
invade Bosigran "with the intention of murdering me and throwing
my body over the cliffs," but the bullies, as they neared their destina-
tion, "gradually melted away, one by one, until only two of them" were
left. The two decided to suspend operations and try again on a more
favorable occasion. Gray believed that if they had known that he was
alone in the house at the time, he would have been slaughtered. "I was
only saved," wrote Gray, "in fact, through the fortunate circumstances
that the malevolence of the Cornish was only exceeded by their
cowardice."[8]  When asked about this mission, Stanley Hocking replied, in a letter of July 14, 1969: "I think this is all nonsense. I never
heard of such an incident, and I would never believe it."[9]

The authorities kept watch of the coastline as the submarine
activities continued. "And at evening," Lawrence wrote in *Kangaroo*,
"when the doors were shut, valiant men lay under the windows to
listen to the conversation in the cosy little room."[10]

"That is true," said Stanley Hocking. "I can show you the very
place. In front of his north window which overlooked one of our little
fields.  Those fellows could have been there in the dark without
Lawrence knowing it, and I firmly believe they were. But he wouldn't
have any occasion to go out there much after dark. I didn't actually see
them, but I think William Henry knew they were keeping a watch. I
should imagine it would have been difficult to hear any conversation
from the sea side of the cottage. They definitely couldn't wait in front
of the cottage because it was a public lane leading down to the farm.
If Lawrence or Frieda had opened the cottage door, watchers on the
lane would have been detected."

Recalling Tregerthen in *Not I, But the Wind*, Frieda Lawrence
remembered the loneliness of the Cornish moors, and how she sometimes thought she could hear the cries of young men calling out to be
saved from the distant battlefields. "I thought how in the past women
like Catherine of Siena had influenced events.  But now what could
any woman do to stem or divert this avalanche?"[11]

"Frieda was very nervous at times," said Stanley Hocking.

"After all, we must remember that she was a German. She had to be very careful. She wouldn't talk about the war with anyone in St. Ives, and she worried about her friends and relatives in Germany. One didn't know what was going to happen then. I think she was rather close with her family in Germany. This reminds me of a day when she and Lawrence were helping us in the harvest field and there was a game going on at sea. German submarines had been there. They had torpedoed some ships only a day or two before. Apparently, a German submarine had been spotted, and it was being hunted by destroyers and airships and patrol boats. There was a grand circle of them, just about a mile offshore on this particular day in August 1917. I remember Frieda saying to me: 'The fools are at it again! What a terrible thing war is! Why must we have wars? In that submarine may be some of the boys I played with as a child, and there they are being hunted to death!' "

"I think Frieda was afraid to show her feelings," said Ivor Short. "The war upset her very much. You see, her husband was nothing more than an Englishman, but her situation was different. I know it was a difficult period for her. I could sense it. And Lawrence was very bitter about being suspected as a spy. He said he was not at fault, but the people wouldn't have it his way."

"I know the coast watchers searched a bag of groceries that Frieda was carrying home from the Zennor shop one day," recalled Stanley Hocking. "They met her on the footpath, and they immediately stopped her. They wanted to know if she had a camera in her shopping bag. One wasn't allowed to take photographs in those days. In fact, I didn't get my camera until several years after the war. Just to be safe. Frieda said she didn't have a camera and showed them the parcel. It was a loaf of bread. She said they looked mighty crestfallen."

Shortly before the Lawrences were ordered out of Cornwall, they visited Cecil Gray on a night when the wind was blowing a gale. The three sat before the fire and amused themselves by singing German folk songs. Suddenly, there was a hammering on the door, and as Gray rose from his chair the door was flung open. Several men with rifles entered and began to search the house. A light had been seen coming from a window. Gray explained that he had no knowledge of the light. What had happened was that the wind had blown loose one of the pins that held the curtain in place. A flicker of light had escaped at irregular intervals like a signal. "Finding nothing incriminating on the premises," wrote Gray, "the intruders withdrew, with operatic gestures like a Verdi chorus, and blood-curdling threats to the effect that I would hear more of the matter."[12] A few days later Gray was summoned to appear in court. It was more serious than he had realized. A German submarine had been reported in the vicinity of Gurnard's Head at the moment the flickering light had been noticed. This, in addition to the singing of German folk songs with his German friend and her husband, placed Gray in an unpleasant predicament.

"Cecil Gray was fined twenty-five pounds," said Stanley Hocking. "I didn't know him very well. He was a stranger like Lawrence and Frieda, and coming amongst us, a bit of suspicion fell on Gray too. In those days it was a very serious matter to show a light when submarines were operating offshore. I think this incident was another reason why the Lawrences were told to leave Cornwall."

In *Not I, But The Wind*, published in 1935, Frieda Lawrence wrote that there was a woman "even now who boasts that she turned us out of Cornwall as spies."[13] Members of the Hocking family were reluctant to discuss this woman who hated the Lawrences, and after they did contribute some details a librarian at the St. Ives Library commented: "I am sure you have discovered many interesting things about D. H. Lawrence, but I would advise you to ignore whatever information you might have concerning the Vicar of Zennor and his daughter." When asked why this should be ignored the librarian's only explanation was "because it is very doubtful if this particular information would prove adequate for your purposes."

"I can't tell you much about the vicar's daughter," said Arthur Eddy, "but I do know that the vicar was suspicious of the Lawrences and the daughter was a gossip. I think she had a lot to say about Frieda. They didn't like Germans in Zennor."

"There was a rumor going about the parson," explained P. O. Eddy. "The word got out that the preacher and his daughter wanted Lawrence to leave Cornwall, and the police went around to check on Lawrence. It was a bit of a secret. All of it. I think the parson distrusted Lawrence, and the parson's daughter talked a bit. The preacher had more distrust than knowledge."

"Look here, this can be traced," said Stanley Hocking. "One can easily find out who the Vicar of Zennor was in 1916 and 1917. I've been warned about this little item. Both the vicar and his daughter are dead, but there are living relatives." When asked if the vicar and Lawrence's postman were the same, Hocking replied: "No, no, they were two

different birds." The subject seemed to make Hocking most uncomfortable, as if he were involved, but when asked why the vicar's
daughter should boast that it was she who got the Lawrences out of
Cornwall, Hocking explained. "One of the chief agitators to get them
out was the vicar. I don't know why entirely. Not exactly. But they
never went to church. If you didn't go to church in those days, you
were considered outside the circle of things. Lawrence was a stranger
in Cornwall and Frieda was a German and they didn't go to church.
All these things worked against them when people began to gossip.
Frieda must have heard locally about this woman—possibly from
some of their literary friends who were still around Cornwall from
time to time after the war. I never had much contact with Lawrence
after he went abroad. But Lawrence knew a little about the vicar before
they went away. I do remember the vicar asked me about the
Lawrences. 'They are Germans, aren't they? What do you know about
them?' "

"Lawrence got after me about the vicar and the church," said
Stanley Hocking after pausing. "I was a lad in the church choir then.
He said to me: 'You go to church on Sunday. Don't you realize that
you're singing a tremendous lot of lies?' I asked him how he made that
out. 'You sing that you believe in the resurrection of the body and life
everlasting, and any intelligent being knows that dead bodies do not
rise again. It would be a terrible thing if they did! What would happen
if all the graves were to open and the dead came trooping back?
Wouldn't it be horrible? Their own friends and family wouldn't want
to see them. What would we do with them?' I've got to admit that I
was rather horrified—his pulling the story of the Bible to pieces."


## XIII


William Henry drove his horse and wagon every Thursday
over the moors to the farmers' market in Penzance. In *Kangaroo*,
Lawrence remembered that "Cornish, magic morning" when he joined
his farm friend and Mabel Hocking for the two-hour ride past Zennor
village and on up the hill where "the barrenness was ancient and
inviolable." It was October 11, 1917. Penzance was buzzing with

rumors, and there was more talk of an invasion. Lawrence did his shopping and then met Mabel at a restaurant. William Henry was to have joined them there too, but he failed to show himself. Lawrence spent the afternoon walking about Penzance. William Henry, "the chatterbox," should have been at the stables at five. "He was an endless gossip, never by any chance punctual." Lawrence and Mabel waited—all the farmers drove home and still no William Henry. It was nearly dark, past seven, before he arrived—"smiling with subtle malevolence and excusing himself so easily."[1] The ostler at the Penzance stable would always say: "Hocking's trap, always the last." The three rode back over the moors as the evening closed in around them. Both Lawrence and Mabel were silent, still irritated for having been kept waiting so long. It was past nine before they reached Eagles Nest. Frieda and Mary Hocking came out of the cottage as the wagon came down the lane. Frieda had spent the afternoon at Gray's and had returned to the cottage just before dark. Higher Tregerthen had been ransacked.

"The authorities just walked in," Stanley Hocking recalled. "Lawrence never locked any doors when he went out. Frieda came down to the farm and told us what had happened. One of my sisters had seen two or three men going up the lane earlier. They were in uniform. But we didn't know the cottage had been searched until Frieda told us. In short, the officials had left things in a hell of a mess. All of Lawrence's letters had been disturbed, and Frieda said that even her workbasket, where she kept her knitting things, had been torn apart and left on the floor. Lawrence told us that they couldn't have found anything because there was nothing to find."

Four men appeared the next morning: an army major, a policeman from St. Ives, and two detectives. Lawrence's college botany notebook and words from a Hebridean song interested the detectives as possible incriminating evidence, and these were seized for further examination. The search continued under bedclothes, into cupboards, and among the dishes in the scullery while Lawrence and Frieda looked on. Then the military officer read his orders from Major General Sir William George Balfour Western, commander of the area. They must leave Cornwall within three days, immediately report to the police wherever they settled, and avoid any coastal region of large ports. When Lawrence asked the major the reason for the notice, he replied: "You know better than I do." Frieda exploded, ready to take the officer to task for "English justice," but Lawrence quickly silenced her.[2]

"I was by the roadside cutting some weeds when the four came by chatting," said Stanley Hocking. "I overheard one of them say: 'That's a job I would rather not have to do.' We never knew the reason why Lawrence was asked to leave Cornwall. Lawrence himself told us that they would not give him a reason for his three-day notice." And did Hocking recall Lawrence's reaction to the notice? "Oh yes. I remember him saying: 'This is hateful! What have I done?' He loved his little cottage in Cornwall. He was perfectly happy here, war or no war, and he didn't have enough money to go traveling elsewhere. 'I am not a spy,' he said. 'I leave it to dirtier people! What is there to spy on here? I am no more guilty than the rabbits in the fields.' Rabbits used to come out right in front of his back window, and Lawrence would watch them playing in the early morning."

Considering the expulsion from a military point of view, it is surprising that the order wasn't delivered earlier. The local police, coast watchers, and military have been criticized repeatedly for their conduct throughout the Cornish episode, and spokesmen of Lawrence's life have been quick to accuse the authorities of being insensitive and cruel. Were the two hounded, spied upon, and bullied for no reason at all? Lawrence and Frieda were strangers who moved to a coastal region just before submarine activity became alarmingly effective, Frieda was German, she was related to the Red Baron, Lawrence was the author of *The Prussian Officer and Other Stories*, his book *The Rainbow* had been reviewed as being unpatriotic, they both read German newspapers, they sang German songs, she sometimes proudly dressed in a German folk costume, he sometimes spoke and wrote of revolution and initiating disruptive campaigns, and they both were with Cecil Gray when the light was seen flickering.

Lawrence and Frieda never violated any of the restrictions imposed on civilians during the time in Cornwall and they minded their own business and they willingly gave information when questioned. But they did arouse suspicion. Their presence was a nuisance to the authorities who had the responsibility of guarding miles of coast. It was easier to expel this couple than to waste valuable manpower. In a letter to Cecil Gray shortly after their arrival in London, Lawrence wrote: "We reported to police here—they had heard nothing about us, and were not in the least interested—couldn't quite see why we report at all. It is evident they work none too smoothly with the military."[3]

But the London police soon became wary. A man from the

Criminal Investigation Department was often seen watching the flat in Earl's Court where the Lawrences were staying, and on one visit Cecil Gray was rudely questioned by the official until Gray lost his patience and told the man to leave. Even in Dollie Radford's Berkshire cottage where the Lawrences retreated the surveillance continued, and a detective had gone to Ernest Weekley to see if the professor had any information to lodge against his former wife. If the injured ex-husband had been a revengeful person, he could have told the detective how Frieda once saw their son, Charles Montague Weekley, in an Officers' Training Corps uniform, and astonished the young man by saying: "Let me hide you somewhere in a cave or in a wood. I don't want you to go and fight. I don't want you to be killed in this stupid war."[4]

Both P. O. Eddy and Stanley Hocking believed that the reason the Lawrences were still being watched after leaving Cornwall was the vicar and his daughter. "Those two had a lot of distrust in them," declared Eddy, and Hocking observed: "They very well may have contacted the police in London." Even Lawrence felt there was a Zennor connection. In a letter to Lady Cynthia Asquith, on December 11, 1917, Lawrence wrote: "It is quite evident that somebody from Cornwall—somebody we don't know, probably—is writing letters to these various departments—and we are being followed everywhere by the persecution."[5]

Several people in Zennor became more suspicious of Cecil Gray after the Lawrences were ordered to leave the area. Perhaps the mood in the village would have turned uglier had the local patriots known that Philip Heseltine's sudden disappearance in the summer of 1917 was the result of a summons to stand for another physical examination. Heseltine had a medical certificate for a nervous disorder, but he ignored the summons and fled to Ireland. Gray, too, had been declared unfit, and by the time he was called up again, in August 1918, he had gone into hiding. He spent the last few months of the war studying in the reading room of the British Museum.

It was a bitter time for Lawrence as he and Frieda began to pack their belongings to leave Tregerthen. He had loved the place so much, and in spite of local suspicion he had made friends with people he would miss. There were the Berrymans, the Hockings, the Shorts, and he had met and liked the Shorts' daughter, Irene Whittley, and her husband Percy. The packing was done in such a rush. Lawrence built a roaring fire with old manuscripts, but at the last moment he had decided to leave his books on the shelves. He was determined to come back. In the midst of their packing, on their last day at Higher Tregerthen, Mary and Mabel Hocking came with dinner from the farm table. In *Kangaroo*, Lawrence recalled how he hated saying farewell to the Hockings—he was so fond of them all: "Only one was not there— the Uncle James. (Uncle Henry) Many a time Somers wondered why Uncle James had gone down the fields, so as not to say good-bye."[6]

Uncle Henry did indeed go down by the cliff so as not to say good-bye. A detail that Lawrence biographer Harry T. Moore noted in *The Priest of Love*: "William Henry Hocking, who had been one of the candidates for *Blutbruderschaft*, drove them to the station; he had become cautious, and some of his family avoided saying farewell to the departing exiles."[7] In a letter of August 2, 1969, Stanley Hocking wrote, after having read Moore's account of the leave-taking: "That's all nonsense. I don't know how Moore could make such a statement about my brother and dear Uncle Henry."[8]

William Henry loved to tell stories to his cronies on market day in Penzance, and more than once he had bragged about the man who wrote books and his wife who was a German baroness. But someone to whom he chatted had little sympathy for the bearded man and Germans. "William Henry said something about Frieda being Ger- man," recalled P. O. Eddy, "and the police came over to the farm and questioned him. I think the police warned him that he could be locked up." The visit from the authorities worried Hocking, and though the friendship continued the farmer was more careful when peddling butter and eggs in Penzance. He had seen men listening under Lawrence's window, and he was afraid that he was under suspicion too. Hocking was unable to hide his fears. In a letter to Robert Mountsier, December 9, 1920, Lawrence wrote: "Of Wm. Henry—he is married, with two little girls, prosperous in money—but household not happy—Mrs. Hocking ill and miserable. I don't hear from them direct. I think Wm. H. was scared when we were kicked out of Zennor and you were a 'Spy'."[9]

"On the day they left," said Stanley Hocking, "they came down to the farm. It was all in such a hurry. I remember my mother giving them some milk and sandwiches to take on the train because it was going to be a rather long journey. I'm not certain, but I believe that William Henry gave them a little money to help them along. I know my Uncle Henry was very sorry that Lawrence had to go. He just couldn't say good-bye. Uncle Henry thought it was a shame that

Lawrence had received notice to clear out. My uncle liked Lawrence, and he thought Frieda was a very nice lady. He liked Frieda very much. Lawrence did say he would be back to live at Tregerthen. But he never did, poor fellow. William Henry drove them to St. Ives station in the trap and I took the big luggage in the market trap. A military officer and a police sergeant were there at the station to see that they got on the train. I remember that. The officials just stood there and said nothing. Nobody spoke. All those people are dead now. Fifty years ago."

William Henry Hocking kept a small diary, which is now in the hands of his son, H. H. Hocking. Hocking explained: "Father started it in 1914. The diary is just notes that my father would refer to over a period of years to see what he had done on the fields. There is only one entry concerning Lawrence." When asked what the entry was, Hocking replied: "October 15, 1917. To St. Ives—Lawrence."

## Notes

### I

[1]D. H. Lawrence, "To John Middleton Murry and Katherine Mansfield," 8 March 1916, letter 1202 of *The Letters of D. H. Lawrence*, ed. George J. Zytaruk and James T. Boulton, 7 vols. (Cambridge: Cambridge UP, 1981), II:569-570.

[2]John Middleton Murry, *Between Two Worlds: An Autobiography* (New York: Julian Messner, 1936), 401-402.

[3]DHL, *Letters*, II:576.

[4]Frieda Lawrence, *Not I, But the Wind* (New York: Viking, 1934), 85.

[5]Murry, *Between Two Worlds*, 403-405.

### II

[1]Murry, *Between Two Worlds*, 261.

[2]Murry, *Between Two Worlds*, 262.

[3]Murry, *Between Two Worlds*, 286-290.

[4]D. H. Lawrence "To John Middleton Murry," 20 May 1929, *The Collected Letters of D. H. Lawrence*, ed. Harry T. Moore, 2 vols. (London: Wm. Heinemann Ltd., 1965), 2:1154.

[5]Murry, *Between Two Worlds*, 286-290.

[6]Mabel Dodge Luhan, *Lorenzo in Taos* (New York: Knopf, 1932), 47.

[7]Murry, *Between Two Worlds*, 321.

[8]F. Lawrence, *Not I, But the Wind*, 85.

[9]Murry, *Between Two Worlds*, 322-338.

[10]Harry T. Moore, *The Priest of Love* (*The Intelligent Heart* revised) (New York: Farrar, Straus and Giroux, 1974), 507.

[11]Ada Lawrence Clarke, "Letter to the Editor," *Everyman*, May 14, 1934.

### III

[1]DHL, *Letters*, II:602.

[2]Katherine Mansfield "To S. S. Koteliansky," 11 May 1916, *Letters*, ed. John Middleton Murry (New York: Knopf, 1941), 61.

[3]Murry, *Between Two Worlds*, 403-405.

[4]Murry, *Between Two Worlds*, 406.

[5]F. Lawrence, *Not I, But the Wind*, 85-86.

[6]Luhan, *Lorenzo in Taos*, 86-91.

[7]DHL, *Letters*, III:302.

[8]Frieda Lawrence, *Frieda Lawrence: The Memoirs and Correspondence*, ed. E. W. Tedlock, Jr. (New York: Knopf, 1964), 158.

[9]Catherine Carswell, *The Savage Pilgrimage: A Narrative of D. H. Lawrence* (New York: Harcourt, Brace, 1932), 73-77.

[10]Carswell, *The Savage Pilgrimage*, 73-77

[11]Louis Untermeyer, from *D. H. Lawrence: A Composite Biography*, ed. Edward Nehls,Vol. 3 (Madison, Wisconsin: University of Wisconsin, 1957-59), 102-103.

[12]David Garnett, "Frieda and Lawrence," from *D. H. Lawrence: Novelist, Poet, Prophet*, ed. Stephen Spender (New York: Harper & Row, 1973), 39.

[13]Emile Delavenay, "Making Another Lawrence," from *The D. H. Lawrence Review*, vol. 8, no. 1, Spring 1975, 84-85.

[14]DHL, *Collected Letters*, I:160.

[15]F. Lawrence, *Not I, But the Wind*, 57.

[16]Diana Trilling, "Letter to a Young Critic," Introduction to *Selected Letters of D. H. Lawrence* (Garden City, New York: Anchor Books, 1961), xviii.

[17]Trilling, *Selected Letters*, xviii.

[18]Cecily Lambert Minchin, from *D. H. Lawrence: A Composite Biography*, 1:465.

[19]DHL, *Collected Letters*, 2:763.

## IV

[1]Murry, *Between Two Worlds*, 403-405.

[2]Murry, *Between Two Worlds*, 408.

[3]Jeffrey Meyers, *Katherine Mansfield* (New York: New Directions, 1978), 82.

[4]Moore, *The Priest of Love*, 260.

[5]Murry, *Between Two Worlds*, 409.

[6]D. H. Lawrence, *Women in Love* (Harmondsworth, England: Penguin, 1964), 397-398.

[7]Murry, *Between Two Worlds*, 412.

[8]Lawrence, *Women in Love*, "Gladiatorial", Chapter 20.

[9]Lawrence, *Women in Love*, 541.

[10]Moore, *The Priest of Love*, 59.

[11]Emile Delavenay, letter to C. J. Stevens, June 20, 1969.

[12]Cecil Gray, *Peter Warlock: A Memoir of Philip Heseltine*, The Life and Letters Series No. 84 (London: Jonathan Cape, 1938), 114.

[13]Idella Purnell Stone, in *D. H. Lawrence: A Composite Biography*, 2:251&506.

[14]F. Lawrence, *Frieda Lawrence: The Memoirs and Correspondence*, 332.

[15]Meyers, *Katherine Mansfield*, 82-83.
[16]DHL, *Letters*, II:115.
[17]Moore, *The Priest of Love*, 541.
[18]DHL, *Collected Letters*, 2:1100.
[19]D. H. Lawrence, *The White Peacock* (Harmondsworth, England: Penguin, 1968), 257.
[20]D. H. Lawrence, *Phoenix II: The Uncollected, Unpublished, and Other Prose Works of D. H. Lawrence*, eds. Warren Roberts and Harry T. Moore (New York: Viking, 1971), 103-107.
[21]DHL, *Phoenix II*, 103-107.
[22]Moore, *The Priest of Love*, 278.
[23]Moore, *The Priest of Love*, 278.
[24]DHL, *Letters*, II:323.
[25]Moore, *The Priest of Love*, 441.
[26]Murry, *Between Two Worlds*, 415.
[27]Murry, *Between Two Worlds*, 408-417.
[28]Murry, *Between Two Worlds*, 417.

V

[1]DHL, *Letters*, II:609.
[2]D. H. Lawrence, *Kangaroo* (Harmondsworth, England: Penguin, 1968), 247.
[3]DHL, *Letters*, II:610.
[4]DHL, *Letters*, II:610.
[5]DHL, *Letters*, II:616-617.
[6]DHL, *Letters*, II:625.
[7]DHL, *Letters*, II:624.
[8]DHL, *Letters*, II:631-632.
[9]Murry, *Between Two Worlds*, 423-424.
[10]Katherine Mansfield, *Letters*, 64-65.
[11]DHL, *Letters*, II:637.
[12]DHL, *Letters*, II:507.
[13]DHL, *Letters*, II:646.
[14]Murry, *Between Two Worlds*, 424.
[15]Lawrence, *Kangaroo*, 264.

VI

[1]Brenda Hamiliton and Tony Soper, "Telediphone Conversation with the Hocking family," BBC, Bristol Branch, in *D. H. Lawrence: A Composite Biography*, 1:365-367.

[2]Lawrence, *Kangaroo*, 262.
[3]DHL, *Letters*, II:642-43.
[4]Lawrence, *Kangaroo*, 264.
[5]DHL, *Letters*, II:647.
[6]DHL, *Letters*, II:652.
[7]D. H. Lawrence, *The Letters of D. H. Lawrence*, eds. James T. Boulton and Andrew Robertson, vol. III (New York: Cambridge University Press, 1984), 173.
[8]DHL, *Letters*, III:179.
[9]DHL, *Letters*, III:261.
[10]DHL, *Letters*, II:663-664.
[11]Unidentified reporter, *The Cornishman*, August 30, 1956.

VII

[1]Carswell, *The Savage Pilgrimage*, 69.
[2]Carswell, *The Savage Pilgrimage*, 69.
[3]Carswell, *The Savage Pilgrimage*, 79-81.
[4]Giuseppe Orioli, *Adventures of a Bookseller* (New York: McBride, 1938) 232-234.
[5]Carswell, *The Savage Pilgrimage*, 84.
[6]John Middleton Murry, *Reminiscences of D. H. Lawrence* (London: Jonathan Cape, 1933), 86-87.
[7]DHL, *Letters*, II:656.
[8]DHL, *Letters*, II:658.
[9]DHL, *Letters*, II:662.
[10]Emile Delavenay "Making Another Lawrence," *The D. H. Lawrence Review*, Vol. 8, No. 1, Spring 1975, 83.
[11]DHL, *Letters*, II:665.
[12]DHL, *Letters*, III:23.
[13]DHL, *Letters*, III:37.
[14]DHL, *Letters*, III:40.
[15]D. H. Lawrence, *Phoenix: The Posthumous Papers of D. H. Lawrence*, ed. Edward D. McDonald (New York: The Viking Press, 1968), 677-679.
[16]D. H. Lawrence, *Selected Poems of D. H. Lawrence*, ed. James Reeves (London: Wm. Heinemann, 1967), 51-53.
[17]Moore, *The Priest of Love*, 318-320.
[18]DHL, *Letters*, III:41.
[19]Lawrence, *Women in Love*, 117.
[20]Moore, *The Priest of Love*, 264.
[21]Lawrence, *Women in Love*, 328.
[22]DHL, *Letters*, III:44.
[23]DHL, *Letters*, III:46.
[24]DHL, *Letters*, III:48.
[25]DHL, *Letters*, III:49.

[26]DHL, *Letters*, III:53-54.
[27]DHL, *Letters*, III:59.
[28]DHL, *Letters*, III:57.
[29]DHL, *Letters*, III:64.


## VIII

[1]DHL, *Letters*, III:69-70.
[2]DHL, *Letters*, III:90.
[3]DHL, *Letters*, III:80-81.
[4]Mrs. Igor Vinogradoff, In *D. H. Lawrence: A Composite Biography*, 1:310.
[5]DHL, *Letters*, III:85.
[6]James Douglas, *Star*, October 22, 1915.
[7]Clement Shorter, *Sphere*, October 23, 1915.
[8]J. C. Squires as Solomon Eagle, *New Statesman*, November 20, 1915.
[9]Methuen to J. B. Pinker (DHL's publisher to DHL's literary agent) September 27, 1915.
[10]D. H. Lawrence, *The Rainbow* (Harmondsworth, England: Penguin, 1968), 311.
[11]DHL, *Letters*, III:87.
[12]DHL, *Letters*, III:91.
[13]DHL, *Letters*, III:95.
[14]Gray, *Peter Warlock*, 220.
[15]W. Charles Pilley, "On Women in Love," *John Bull*, September 17, 1921.
[16]Gray, *Peter Warlock*, 220-231.
[17]DHL, *Letters*, III:102.
[18]DHL, *Letters*, III:103.
[19]DHL, *Letters*, III:109.
[20]Dr. Muriel Radford, in *D. H. Lawrence: A Composite Biography*, I:414.
[21]Moore, *The Priest of Love*, 277.
[22]DHL, *Collected Letters*, 2:730.
[23]Luhan, *Lorenzo in Taos*, 40-43.
[24]DHL, *Letters*, III:53-54.


## IX

[1]DHL, *Kangaroo*, 257.
[2]DHL, *Kangaroo*, 262.
[3]Raul Mirenda, in *DHL: A Composite Biography*, 3:61.
[4]DHL, *Kangaroo*, 257.

## X

[1]DHL, *Letters*, III:124.
[2]DHL, *Letters*, III:127.
[3]Cecil Gray, *Musical Chairs, or Between Two Stools* (London: Home & Van Thal, 1948), 126.
[4]DHL, *Letters*, III:130.
[5]DHL, *Letters*, III:133-134.
[6]DHL, *Letters*, III:134.
[7]DHL, *Letters*, III:135.
[8]DHL, *Letters*, III:136.
[9]Gray, *Musical Chairs*, 126.
[10]DHL, *Letters*, III:138.
[11]DHL, *Letters*, III:224.
[12]Carswell, *The Savage Pilgrimage*, 276-277.
[13]Gray, *Musical Chairs*, 131-140.
[14]DHL, *Letters*, III:173.
[15]Barbara Guest, *Herself Defined: The Poet H. D. and her World* (Garden City, New York: Doubleday & Company, Inc., 1984), 89.
[16]DHL, *Letters*, III:178.
[17]Lawrence, *Kangaroo*, 266.
[18]Gray, *Musical Chairs*, 131-140.
[19]DHL, *Letters*, III:180.
[20]DHL, *Letters*, III:142-144.
[21]Chatto & Windus to J. B. Pinker, in DHL, *Letters*, July 18, 1917, III:145.
[22]DHL, *Letters*, III:152.
[23]DHL, *Letters*, III:153.
[24]DHL, *Letters*, III:154.
[25]DHL, *Letters*, III:158.
[26]DHL, *Letters*, III:162-163.

## XI

[1]DHL, *Letters*, II:211.
[2]DHL, *Letters*, II:340.
[3]DHL, *Letters*, III:32.
[4]DHL, *Letters*, III:215.
[5]Violet Hunt, *I Have This to Say: The Story of my Flurried Years* (New York: Boni & Liveright, 1926), 259-260.
[6]David Garnett, *The Flowers of the Forest* (New York: Harcourt, 1956), 3-5.
[7]Emile Delavenay, *The D. H. Lawrence Review*, Vol. 8, No. 1, 86.
[8]John Maynard Keynes, in *D. H. Lawrence: A Composite Biography*, 1:286.
[9]DHL, *Letters*, II:320-321.
[10]DHL, *Letters*, II:546-547.
[11]Bertrand Russell, in *Harper's Magazine*, CCVI, No. 1233, February 1953, 93-95.

[12]Moore, *The Priest of Love*, 231.
[13]Emile Delavenay, in *The D. H. Lawrence Review*, Vol. 8, No. 1, 87.
[14]Lawrence, *Kangaroo*, 240.
[15]DHL, *Letters*, II:486-487.

## XII

[1]Lawrence, *Kangaroo*, 258.
[2]Moore, *The Priest of Love*, 279-280.
[3]Gray, *Musical Chairs*, 128-131.
[4]Lawrence, *Kangaroo*, 251.
[5]Lawrence, *Kangaroo*, 253.
[6]Gray, *Musical Chairs*, 126-131.
[7]Gray, *Musical Chairs*, 126-131.
[8]Gray, *Musical Chairs*, 126-131.
[9]Stanley Hocking, letter to C. J. Stevens, July 14, 1969.
[10]Lawrence, *Kangaroo*, 252.
[11]F. Lawrence, *Not I, But the Wind*, 88.
[12]Gray, *Musical Chairs*, 126-128.
[13]F. Lawrence, *Not I, But the Wind*, 80.

## XIII

[1]Lawrence, *Kangaroo*, 265-266.
[2]Moore, *The Priest of Love*, 281.
[3]DHL, *Letters*, III:170.
[4]F. Lawrence, *Not I, But the Wind*, 92.
[5]DHL, *Letters*, III:188.
[6]Lawrence, *Kangaroo*, 274.
[7]Moore, *The Priest of Love*, 281.
[8]Stanley Hocking, letter to C. J. Stevens, August 2, 1969.
[9]DHL, *Letters*, III:634.

Selected Bibliography

Albright, Daniel. *Personality and Impersonality: Lawrence, Woolf, and Mann.* Chicago: University of Chicago Press, 1978.

Aldington, Richard. *Portrait of a Genius, But.* New York: Duell, Sloan & Pearce, 1950.

Alldritt, Keith. *The Visual Imagination of D. H. Lawrence.* Evanston, Illinois: Northwestern University Press, 1971.

Andrews, W. T., ed. *Critics on D. H. Lawrence.* Coral Gables, Florida: University of Miami Press, 1971.

Beal, Anthony. *D. H. Lawrence.* New York: Grove, 1961.

Brewster, Earl and Achsah. *D. H. Lawrence: Reminiscences and Correspondences.* London: Secker, 1934.

Bynner, Witter. *Journey with Genius: Recollections and Reflections Concerning the D. H. Lawrences.* New York: Day, 1951.

Callow, Philip. *Son and Lover: The Younger D. H. Lawrence.* New York: Stein & Day, 1975.

Carswell, Catherine. *The Savage Pilgrimage: A Narrative of D. H. Lawrence.* New York: Harcourt, Brace, 1932.

Cavitch, David. *D. H. Lawrence and the New World.* London: Oxford University Press, 1969.

Chambers, Jessie. *D. H. Lawrence: A Personal Record,* by E. T. New York: Barnes & Noble, 1965.

Clarke, Colin. *River of Dissolution: D. H. Lawrence and English Romanticism.* New York: Barnes & Noble, 1969.

Daleski, H. M. *The Forked Flame: A Study of D. H. Lawrence.* London: Faber and Faber, 1965.

Delany, Paul. *D. H. Lawrence's Nightmare: The Writer and His Circle in the Years of the Great War.* New York: Basic Books, 1978.

Delavenay, Emile. *D. H. Lawrence: The Man and His Work: The Formative Years: 1885-1919*. Carbondale, Illinois: Southern Illinois University Press, 1972.

—, "Making Another Lawrence." *The D. H. Lawrence Review*. Vol. 8, No. 1, Spring 1975.

Douglas, James. *Star*. October 22, 1915.

Draper, R. P. *D. H. Lawrence: The Critical Heritage*. London: Routledge & Kegan Paul, 1970.

Foster, Joseph. *D. H. Lawrence in Taos*. Albuquerque, New Mexico: University of New Mexico Press, 1972.

Freeman, Mary. *D. H. Lawrence: A Basic Study of His Ideas*. Gainesville, Florida: University of Florida Press, 1955.

Garnett, David. *The Flowers of the Forest*. New York: Harcourt, 1956.

Gordon, Ian A. *Katherine Mansfield*. London: Longmans, Green & Co., 1963.

Gray, Cecil. *Musical Chairs, or Between Two Stools*. London: Home and Van Thal, 1948.

—. *Peter Warlock: A Memoir of Philip Heseltine*. The Life and Letters Series No. 84. London: Jonathan Cape, 1938.

Green, Martin. *The von Richthofen Sisters: The Triumphant and the Tragic Modes of Love*. New York: Basic Books, 1974.

Guest, Barbara. *Herself Defined: The Poet H. D. and Her World*. Garden City, New York: Doubleday & Company, Inc., 1984.

Hahn, Emily. *Lorenzo: D. H. Lawrence and the Women Who Loved Him*. New York and Philadelphia: Lippincott, 1975.

Hamalian, Leo, ed. *D. H. Lawrence: A Collection of Criticism*. New York: McGraw-Hill, 1973.

Hough, Graham. *The Dark Sun: A Study of D. H. Lawrence*. Harmondsworth, England: Penguin, 1961.

Hunt, Violet. *I Have This to Say: The Story of My Flurried Years*. New York: Boni & Liveright, 1926.

Kermode, Frank. *D. H. Lawrence*. New York: Viking Press, 1973.

Lawrence, D. H. *The Collected Letters of D. H. Lawrence*. Volumes 1 & 2, ed. Harry T. Moore. London: Wm. Heinemann Ltd., 1965.

—. *The Complete Short Stories of D. H. Lawrence.* 3 Vols. Harmondsworth, England: Penguin, 1978-1980.

—. *D. H. Lawrence's Letters to Bertrand Russell,* ed. Harry T. Moore. New York: Gotham Book Mart, 1948.

—. *Kangaroo.* Harmondsworth, England: Penguin, 1968.

—. *Lady Chatterley's Lover.* Harmondsworth, England: Penguin, 1968.

—. *The Letters of D. H. Lawrence.* Volumes I, II, and III. New York: Cambridge University Press, 1979, 1981, 1984.

—. *The Letters of D. H. Lawrence,* ed. Aldous Huxley. Harmondsworth, England: Penguin, 1968.

—. *Phoenix: The Posthumous Papers of D. H. Lawrence,* ed. Edward D. McDonald. New York: The Viking Press, 1968.

—. *Phoenix II: Uncollected, Unpublished, and Other Prose Works of D. H. Lawrence,* ed. Warren Roberts and Harry T. Moore. New York: The Viking Press, 1971.

—. *The Plumed Serpent.* Harmondsworth, England: Penguin, 1961.

—. *The Quest for Rananim, D. H. Lawrence's Letters to S. S. Koteliansky, 1914-1930,* ed. George J. Zytaruk. Montreal: McGill Queen's University Press, 1970.

—. *The Rainbow.* Harmondsworth, England: Penguin, 1968.

—. *The Selected Letters of D. H. Lawrence,* ed. with Introduction by Diana Trilling. Garden City, New York: Anchor Books, 1961.

—. *Selected Poems of D. H. Lawrence,* ed. James Reeves. London: Wm. Heinemann, 1967.

—. *Sons and Lovers.* Harmondsworth, England: Penguin, 1967.

—. *Studies in Classic American Literature.* Garden City, New York: Doubleday Anchor Books, 1953.

—. *The White Peacock.* Harmondsworth, England: Penguin, 1968.

—. *Women in Love.* Harmondsworth, England: Penguin, 1969.

Lawrence, Frieda. *Frieda Lawrence: The Memoirs and Correspondence,* ed. E. W. Tedlock, Jr. New York: Knopf, 1964.

—. *Not I, But the Wind.* New York: Viking, 1934.

Leavis, F. R. *D. H. Lawrence: Novelist.* Harmondsworth, England: Penguin, 1964.

Lucas, Robert. *Frieda Lawrence: The Story of Frieda von Richthofen and D. H. Lawrence.* New York: The Viking Press, 1973.

Luhan, Mabel Dodge. *Lorenzo in Taos.* New York: Knopf, 1932.

Mairet, Philip. *John Middleton Murry.* London: Longmans, Green & Co., 1958.

Mansfield, Katherine. *Letters,* ed. J. M. Murry. New York: Knopf, 1941.

Mason, H. A. "Lawrence in Love." *The Cambridge Quarterly.* Vol. IV, No. 2, Spring 1969.

Merrild, Knud. *A Poet and Two Painters: A Memoir of D. H. Lawrence.* Reprinted as *With D. H. Lawrence in New Mexico: A Memoir of D. H. Lawrence.* London: Routledge & Kegan Paul, 1964.

Meyers, Jeffrey. *Homosexuality and Literature 1890-1930.* Montreal: McGill-Queen's University Press, 1977.

—. *Katherine Mansfield.* New York: New Directions, 1978.

Miko, Stephen J. *Toward 'Women in Love': The Emergence of a Lawrentian Aesthetic.* New Haven, Connecticut: Yale University Press, 1971.

Moore, Harry T. *D. H. Lawrence: His Life and Works.* New York: Twayne, 1964.

—. *A D. H. Lawrence Miscellany.* Carbondale, Illinois: Southern Illinois University Press, 1959.

—. *The Intelligent Heart.* New York: Farrar, Straus and Young, 1954.

—. *The Priest of Love.* (*The Intelligent Heart* revised) New York: Farrar, Straus and Giroux, 1974.

Murry, John Middleton. *Reminiscences of D. H. Lawrence.* London: Jonathan Cape, 1933.

—. *Son of Woman: The Story of D. H. Lawrence.* London: Jonathan Cape, 1931.

Nehls, Edward, ed. *D. H. Lawrence: A Composite Biography.* 3 Volumes. Madison, Wisconsin: University of Wisconsin, 1957-1959.

Nin, Anaïs. *D. H. Lawrence: An Unprofessional Study.* Denver, Colorado: Alan Swallow, 1964.

Orioli, Giuseppe. *Adventures of a Bookseller.* New York: McBride, 1938.

Pilley, W. Charles. "Women in Love." *John Bull.* September 17, 1921.

Russell, Bertrand. *Portraits from Memory and Other Essays.* New York: Simon and Schuster, 1956.

Sagar, Keith. *The Art of D. H. Lawrence,* New York: Cambridge University Press, 1966.

—. *D. H. Lawrence: A Calendar of His Work.* Austin, Texas: University of Texas Press, 1979.

Schorer, Mark. *D. H. Lawrence.* New York: Dell, 1968.

Shorter, Clement. *Sphere.* October 23, 1915.

Smith, Anne, ed. *Lawrence and Women.* New York: Barnes & Noble, 1980.

Spender, Stephen, ed. *D. H. Lawrence: Novelist, Poet, Prophet.* New York: Harper & Row, 1973.

Spilka, Mark. *D. H. Lawrence: A Collection of Critical Essays.* Englewood Cliffs, New Jersey: Prentice-Hall, 1963.

—. *The Love Ethic of D. H. Lawrence.* Bloomington, Indiana: Indiana University Press, 1965.

Squires, J. C. as Eagle, Solomon. *New Statesman.* November 20, 1915.

Tiverton, Father William. *D. H. Lawrence and Human Existence.* New York: Philosophical Library, 1951.

Trease, Geoffrey. *The Phoenix and the Flame: D. H. Lawrence.* New York: Viking Press, 1973.

Weiss, Daniel A. *Oedipus in Nottingham: D. H. Lawrence.* Seattle, Washington: Washington University Press, 1962.

Young, Kenneth. *D. H. Lawrence.* London: Longmans, Green & Co., 1966.

# Index